AMPLIFY!

SECRETS FOR SUCCESSFUL SPEAKING

Other Books by

Karen Porter

If You Give A Girl A Giant

Study Guide: If You Give A Girl A Giant

I'll Bring the Chocolate

Speak Like Jesus

Get Ready!

Amplify!

Secrets to Successful Speaking

Karen Porter

Bold Vision Books
PO Box 2011
Friendswood, Texas 77549

©Copyright Karen Porter 2020

ISBN: 978-1946708-533

Library of Congress Control Number: 2020949653

Printed in the U.S.A.

BVB - Bold Vision Books www.boldvisionbooks.com

Published in conjunction with literary agent Janet Grant, Books and Such Literary Agency

Cover Design: Barefaced Creative

Interior Design: kae Creative Solutions

Dedication

To you who communicate up front and stand on the stage

May your words inspire and influence.

"Let my teaching fall like rain and my words descend like dew, like showers on new grass, like abundant rain on tender plants" (Deuteronomy 32:2)

Acknowledgments

Thank you to George Porter who always tells the truth slathered in love and kindness. Life would be empty without you.

Thank you to Euphanel Goad and Nick Goad. Thank you for creating a writing paradise and inviting me to spend time there. Your kindness overflows.

Thank you to Florence Littauer who challenged me and loved me. Most of what I know came from you and now this material is such a part of me that I dare to write it in a book.

Thank you to Carole Lewis for being a friend and mentor and encourager. I'm always filled with joy when I see your name flash on my phone.

Thank you to Carol Kent for being a role model and friend. Your encouragement is gold. I love that we are not competitors because the more ships in the sea makes the water rise.

Thank you to Rhonda Rhea for your spark of life and sunshine. I love working and laughing and planning and scheming with you.

Thank you to all the event planners who believed in me and gave me the opportunity to speak.

ON THE MOUNTAINS OF TRUTH YOU CAN NEVER CLIMB IN VAIN: EITHER YOU WILL REACH A POINT HIGHER UP TODAY, OR YOU WILL BE TRAINING YOUR POWERS SO THAT YOU WILL BE ABLE TO CLIMB HIGHER TOMORROW. ~FRIEDRICH NIETZSCHE

Chapter 20   The Care and Feeding of a Healthy Platform   185

Chapter 21   Blueprints for Team Building   195

Chapter 22   A Cleansing Breath   199

Meet Karen   205

Endnotes   206

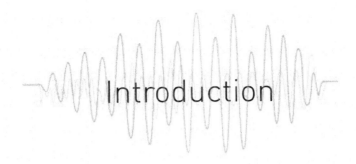

Introduction

"IF I WENT BACK TO COLLEGE AGAIN, I'D CONCENTRATE ON TWO AREAS: LEARNING TO WRITE AND TO SPEAK BEFORE AN AUDIENCE. NOTHING IN LIFE IS MORE IMPORTANT THAN THE ABILITY TO COMMUNICATE EFFECTIVELY." ~GERALD R. FORD

"Great opening illustration!"

"Love the laugh lines."

"Story about the church in England may be over the top—tone it down a bit."

"Outstanding eye contact."

"You said the words 'you know' nine times in one minute."

"Work on the gestures in the middle section of presentation—be more deliberate."

"Be careful of Texas drawl, especially when saying 'you'—sounds like 'yer.'"

"Honest and authentic."

Th, hese are comments I've received when I've worked with a speaker coach. Yes, I am a coach, but I still get coaching. Nothing challenges me more than getting a critique from a professional, and nothing inspires me more than the challenges they give me. I want to be the best I can be on the stage. You do too. That's why you picked up this book.

Let me warn you that being coached forces you to risk. It can be unpleasant, but it can also be fun. Most of all coaching is stimulating. Abraham Lincoln said, "I will study and prepare so that when my time comes, I'll be ready." What about you? Are you ready to get ready?

I hope so because I want to coach you in the pages of this book. Together we are going to discover how to craft a dynamite presentation and how you can present it with power, authenticity, humor, and effectiveness. And without notes. I know these are big promises, but I believe in the tips and strategies—and secrets—in this book.

Your dreams of teaching, preaching, inspiring, or becoming a motivational speaker will be much closer to coming true if you follow these guidelines and discover the secrets of Amplify!

EVERYONE NEEDS A COACH. IT
DOESN'T MATTER WHETHER YOU'RE A
BASKETBALL PLAYER, A TENNIS PLAYER,
A GYMNAST OR A BRIDGE PLAYER.
~BILL GATES

A coach is a guide for your future. As your coach, I'll fix a few places that need repair in your speaking process. Feedback from a coach differs from your friends or your mom reacting or responding to your speaking. They will tell you what they thought and felt. A good coach will show you how to make it better. In these pages, I will give you tips and tools which might be contrary to what others say, but it is the best knowledge and research to date. If you are serious about becoming a professional speaker, learn all you can in this book and put it into practice. Then hire a coach to help you personally. Michael Hyatt said, "If I were starting over today, I'd hire a coach sooner."

Chapter 1
Put a Fine Point on It

If you chase two rabbits, you will not catch either one." ~Russian Proverb

You have been in the audience when the speaker rambles and fumbles, haven't you? You were bored and watching the clock, hoping to see the minutes move fast, but time seemed to be broken. I've been in those audiences and have watched that clock and squirmed in my seat too.

Presenting a powerful and inspiring presentation requires us to put a fine point on it—to find one main idea or one prevailing theme that will captivate the audience.

A common mistake speakers make is trying to say everything about their subject from A to Z. A preacher gives every lesson from Genesis to Revelation. A tech guru over-explains the technology. A motivational expert covers every emotional behavior. A DIY specialist shows projects from the roof to the basement. The audience may feel intrigued, but they don't take away any life-changing insights or practical and useful help for their situation.

Speakers who come to me for coaching typically have too much information in one presentation. Candace presented a 30-minute motivational speech, which was entertaining. She had great stage skills and presented her material with a sparkle. But the presentation contained several topics she had connected loosely. We went to work on the content: dividing, eliminating, organizing, and tweaking. She had four 30-minute presentations—enough for a weekend retreat. Each one of her new presentations focused on a main point with powerful stories and information as support for that point. Each new presentation was potent and persuasive.

"ASK YOURSELF, 'IF I HAD ONLY SIXTY SECONDS ON THE STAGE, WHAT WOULD I ABSOLUTELY HAVE TO SAY TO GET MY MESSAGE ACROSS."
~ JEFF DEWAR

LIKE A BRIDGE

I was traveling in New England noticing the many covered bridges crossing streams and rivers. Several caught my eye for their charm and quaint design. The overwhelming intrigue of the bridge was the other side. Whether a bridge is crossing a valley or a swamp or a river or a stream or a bay, the focus is the one destination. Why would I cross the bridge? The unique and single reason is to go from one state to the other or from one city to the other.

All messages must have a central idea, a theme melody that flows throughout the presentation—an idea that gets your audience across the bridge.

Like a Symphony

If you listen carefully to a symphony, the melody or refrain will appear throughout the performance in various forms and sounds, major and minor keys, different tempos and rhythms. Likewise, your main idea must show up in various forms throughout your sermon, presentation, or speech. Your key point should be one powerful statement or principle. The focal point isn't the title or topic; it is the central theme. You can't cover everything you know in a 30-minute presentation. So choose one crucial point, and make it powerful. The audience will not forget it.

What is Your Point?

Every presentation must have a main point. What is the one over-arching idea you want to make? What one thought do you want your audience to hear? What one action do you expect your audience to take after they have heard your presentation? The answers to these questions are critical and you must answer before you can build a successful presentation.

Think of the main point in terms of a tweetable message. Could you boil your presentation down to a tweet of 280 characters? Could you explain your message in a sentence of ten words or less?

"IF YOU CAN'T EXPLAIN IT SIMPLY, YOU DON'T UNDERSTAND IT WELL ENOUGH."
~ ALBERT EINSTEIN

My mentor and friend, Florence Littauer, trained more than 30,000 speakers, challenging them with two questions, "Do you have anything to say, and does anyone need to hear it?" I'm going to help you answer these questions in the pages of this book. I believe your life experiences are like seeds planted in you throughout your life have given you a message to speak. And you can craft that message so your audience benefits. Your goal is to change lives, whether in the corporate setting or in a faith-based setting.

Discovering our main point forces us to remove the frills, showing our audiences a clear path if they listen to us. Because of this emphasis on the audience and what action they will take, our point becomes more than a theme. Our main point can be new info for the audience to learn; for example, how to use a social media site. Perhaps our over-arching idea is to help the audience change a behavior; for instance, eating healthy foods. Maybe our goal is to help those who hear our presentation think deeply; for example, to leave a powerful legacy, or to model faith in God in life situations.

What will you leave with your audience? A desire to follow God? A challenge to try a new technique? How will you help them become better people because they heard your presentation? What one new insight will they take home to change the way they do business, sell products, minister, work, play, or live?

Score a Point

I speak to corporate audiences, civic groups, church groups, professional organizations, and groups of writers and speakers. Finding the key point for these varied audiences is a challenge. I've discovered some secrets—techniques that help me.

1) **Know the audience.** Ask the event planner basic questions about who will attend the event. What is the average age? Are these attendees working in a corporate

setting or are they entrepreneurs? Are these attendees young moms who are raising kids or are they older women who are empty nesters concerned with life after kids? What are their needs and values? What events in the community will affect the audience (a school shooting, a business closing, an oil discovery, or the local team winning the state championship). Ken Haemer said, "Designing a presentation without an audience in mind is like writing a love letter and addressing it: To Who it May Concern."

2) **Know the event.** Is the event meant to be a time of inspiration that challenges the audience to live fuller lives or is it meant to be a time of fun and laughter? What else is on the program at the event—such as a business meeting, an induction of new officers, a style show, or a musical group performance? Should your presentation be strictly biblical or informational in content, or should you tell your personal inspirational story?

3) **Define Your Message.** As you become more advanced in speaking, you will develop a style and a central message. When you do, incorporate that central message into every presentation. If your key focus is joy, for example, include joy into every message. If your theme is organization and productivity, bring out the importance of these tools no matter what your topic. Harvey Diamond said, "If you don't know what you want to achieve in your presentation your audience never will."

4) **Answer the question,** "So what?" You can give your audience facts, statistics, and information, but how does it help these individuals? You can tell your story, but what does it mean for the hearer? When you answer the question, "so what," you will find your main point and your takeaway. Your goal is for your audience to say, "me too."

The iconic Golden Gate Bridge spans nearly two miles across

San Francisco Bay, connecting San Francisco to its northern neighbors in Marin County. The bridge is an engineering marvel and the most photographed bridge in the world. Its art deco towers, innovative suspension cables, and paint color, dubbed "international orange," are famous worldwide. We could talk about the beauty and construction genius of the bridge for hours, but the most important fact about the bridge is that it is crossed by more than 45 million vehicles each year. The bridge is in place so people can get to their destination.

Your main point in your presentation is like a bridge. It is the path you take your audience through to get to the conclusion you planned or the result you hoped for. For each presentation, design one main point. What is the one reason for your speech?

Try writing the key point of your presentation in one sentence of 15 words or less.

In my talk about women's friendships being like chocolate, my main point is: **All the luscious qualities of friendship are like all the luscious qualities of chocolate.**

I often speak about my book *If You Give A Girl A Giant.* My main point is: **God gives us unlikely weapons to slay the giants of discouragement, defeat, fear, and self."**

My presentations on the personalities is titled: Why Can't You Be Normal Like Me? The focal point for that talk is: **Karen will help your group learn to get along with difficult people.**

When you develop a main-message sentence of 15 words or

less, you have condensed the topic into a bite of information that will help you stay focused while you speak. And if you are single-minded, your audience will also concentrate on the message.

"THERE ARE THREE TARGETS TO AIM
AT IN PUBLIC SPEAKING: FIRST, TO
GET INTO YOUR SUBJECT, THEN TO
GET YOUR SUBJECT INTO YOURSELF,
AND LASTLY, TO GET YOUR SUBJECT
INTO THE HEART OF YOUR AUDIENCE."
~ALEXANDER GREGG

Chapter 2
Not Your Mother's Outline

"When speaking in public, your message — no matter how important — will not be effective or memorable if you don't have a clear structure." ~ Patricia Fripp

Once you have decided on your bridge, it is time to add supports. The supports give you confidence to reach your destination. Your main topic will help your hearers know what you want them to know, and the supports will provide proof and confidence in your message.

Find two to four major statements or ideas that support your key point. These supports are strong evidence for your main thought and will transport your listeners toward understanding and applying the message you present.

You may wonder why only one main point and a few sub points is important. Because sometimes a presentation may go wrong or flat despite your best efforts. Your mind might go blank in the middle of your talk. Maybe all the lights and electric suddenly shut off in the middle of your talk, but then came back on just as suddenly. A myriad of unexpected distractions can happen during a presentation. So be ready with a major point and a few sub-points that you can return to regardless of disturbances or interruptions. And because your audience can follow your logic and presentation better if there is a good structure.

"THE AUDIENCE ONLY PAYS ATTENTION AS LONG AS YOU KNOW WHERE YOU ARE GOING." ~PHILLIP CROSBY

FOCUS

Someone said, "Your brain begins working on the day you are born and never stops—until you get up to speak in public. Then it quits." Funny words, but truer than we want to believe. It is so easy to get off the central message and follow a trail to another subject—just in time to discover you have used all your time and didn't cover the main message.

Focus isn't as hard as you might think if you know your main point and then build your supports into an outline that both you and your audience can remember. The power and charm of your message depends on the relevance of your main point and the strength of your supports. The supports list your sub-points in outline form.

OUTLINE FRAMEWORK

Remember the outline techniques your eighth-grade English teacher taught. Roman numeral I followed by capital A followed by numeric 1 followed by small a. These techniques are not helpful when preparing an outline for your supports. What you need, instead, is a framework—a skeleton where you can hang the flesh of your message. And that framework must be simple and interesting—and easily remembered while you are on stage.

One of the best compliments you can receive as a speaker is for someone in your audience to repeat your outline back to you. The outline in one of my presentations is "Attitude, Gratitude, Certitude." The rhyming outline is easy to remember, and I usually repeat it several times throughout the message. For example, "Not only do you need a great attitude, but you also need gratitude." And "Attitude and gratitude aren't enough; one more characteristic will make life a success—certitude." The audience picks up on the rhyme and the rhythm of the words, and when someone comes to me after the presentation and repeats the outline, I consider the day a great success.

Learn to connect the points of the outline without using numbers. Use a connector sentence instead of saying, "My second point is … " or "Second … " Repeat the first point to lead into the second point. Repeat outline points number one and two to set up point number three without saying the numbers.

"If you pray simply and deeply, (points one and two), you can pray freely (point three)."

"God asks you to Trust Him (point one) and He also asks you to Obey Him (point two)."

Using this technique reminds your audience of all the supports you've used and keeps these points in their minds as they process the main idea (the bridge) of your presentation.

When I speak about Goliath's four brothers—who represent the giants who come at us in life—I transition between the giants by making a transition connection and by comparing the two.

"We face the giant of discouragement in life's disappointments, but when a sudden event or tragedy happens, the giant of defeat enters. What is the difference between discouragement and defeat? One knocks you down; the other knocks you out."

REMEMBER IT

The first key to speaking without notes is developing an outline you can remember. One of my favorite outlines came from superstar singer Reba McIntyre who spoke about living life to the full. She said we need a "Back Bone, a Funny Bone, and a Wish Bone." I wish I had thought of that outline because it would be easy to remember on stage and the depth of each point is fertile— not to mention amusing and entertaining.

A great outline that is an easy-to-remember blueprint for your speech will allow you to put your notes away and speak directly to your audience. If your outline is easy for you to recall, it will be easy for your audience to follow. The PIER technique that I will teach you in a later chapter will show you how to speak without notes, but freedom on the stage begins with a fabulous outline.

You can develop clever outlines that you and your audience will remember. Begin by understanding different outline styles. Then you can build the most successful outline for your presentation.

Rhyme/Resonance—Choose words with echoing sounds and similar tone. Notice the ending sound of each of these outline points.

MAIN POINT: HOW TO LEARN TO PLAY THE PIANO.

Skill

Will

Thrill

****

MAIN POINT: CAN YOU BECOME AN ENTREPRENEUR?

Are You an Administrator?

Are You a Contractor?

Are You a Promoter?

* *

MAIN POINT: GIVING THE PERFECT DINNER PARTY

Planning

Cooking

Enjoying

* *

MAIN POINT: PRAYING CONSISTENTLY AND WITH POWER IS POSSIBLE

If You Pray Simply

If You Pray Deeply

If You Pray Freely

* *

Action Verbs—Help your audience achieve a goal or give them instructions using verbs that call for a response.

MAIN POINT: DEVELOPING LEADERSHIP QUALITIES

Take Action in the Absence of Orders

Develop a Plan for Success

Become the Most Dependable Team Member

Let Your Enthusiasm Take the Lead

* *

Main Point: Getting Along with Difficult People Depends on You

Answer Harsh Words Kindly

Offer Sympathy Freely

Give Advice Thoughtfully

* *

Main Point: What God Asks of Each Person

Trust

Obey

* *

Alliteration—Begin each point in the outline with the same letter.

Main Point: Stop the Busyness and Keep the Good Life

Learn to Say No

Leave the Unimportant Behind

Love People More than Stuff

* *

Main Point: So You Want to Write a Novel

Attend a Conference

Accept Constructive Criticism

Avoid Confusing Comments

* *

Main Point: Discover Your True Identity

Authentic

Able

* *

Questions—Use an inquiry to address a problem or obtain a response.

Main Point: Two Days to Productivity

What Will You Do Today?

What Will You Do Tomorrow?

* *

Main Point: Powerful Words Prove We Care

Does God Care How We Speak?

Do People Care What We Say?

Do We Care What Words We Utter?

* *

Sentences—Use whole thoughts expressed with noun, verb, and phrases. These outlines are often combined with alliteration, repetition, or rhyming.

MAIN POINT: LEAVING A LEGACY

When You Build Up Others, You Leave A Legacy of Encouragement.

When You Hear What Others Say, You Leave a Legacy of Listening

When You Read and Memorize Scripture, You Leave a Legacy of the Word

* *

MAIN POINT: THE STORY OF THE WOMAN WITH ALABASTER BOX SHOWS US HOW TO LIVE

Humble and Empty Myself

Draw Near and Offer All

Fill Up with Jesus and Live in Holy Expectation

* *

Acrostics—Choose a central word of the speech and use the first letter to form the outline.

MAIN POINT: LIVING WITH HOPE

H—Helping Others with our Hands

O—Offering Peace with our Words

P—Placing Trust with our Minds

E—Extending Faith with our Hearts

* *

Main Point: Finding JOY in Life

J—Jealousy Removed

O—Offenses Forgiven

Y—Youthfulness Restored

* *

Pictures or other visuals—Use a visual to depict the outline.

A photo of a file cabinet would allow you to use the parts of the cabinet as your outline:

Main Point: Living with Stuff

Drawers – What is Important Enough to keep?

File Folders – Organizing Your Life

Lock – Protecting Yourself

* *

A photo of a highway would allow you to use parts of the road as your outline.

Main Point: Traveling through Life with Purpose

Solid Foundation

Road Signs

Middle Line

Keep Moving

* * * * * * * * * * * * * * * * * * * *

How to…— Offer techniques to accomplish a task. Numbers are effective when used in the title of a "How to" topic.

MAIN POINT: THREE KEYS TO BUILDING A PROJECT TEAM

Choose the Right People

Meet Regularly

Learn Technology Tools

* * * * * * * * * * * * * * * * * * * *

MAIN POINT: FOUR WAYS TO BUILD A SPEECH

Determine the Main Point

Structure an Outline

Add Illustrations and Examples

Enhance with Sources

* * * * * * * * * * * * * * * * * * * *

Chart—Use a diagram or map to direct the audience's attention.

Instead of listing the points, use a photo of stair steps to teach a skill.

MAIN POINT: HOW TO SET UP YOUR ACCOUNT ON FACEBOOK.

Step One: Set up Your Computer

Step Two: Download the App

Step Three: Create a Sign-in Name and Avatar

A diagram of the body would be an interesting way to outline 1 John 1:1:

MAIN POINT: HOW TO KNOW JESUS

Ears: We have Heard.

Eyes: We have Seen.

Hands: We have Touched.

Lists—Prepare a list of thoughts or actions to motivate your audience.

MAIN POINT: LEARNING THE BASICS OF FAITH.

Faith is Taking the First Step When You Can't See the Way.

Faith is Being Sure That God is in Control.

Faith is Placing Your Future in God's Hands.

* *

Comparison/Contrast—Use similar or contradictory objects or terms to prove your main theme.

Before / After

Now / Later

Eat Veggies / Shun Sugar

* *

Scripture—The words in the verses form the outline.

Galatians 1:3

Grace and Peace – from God to you

* *

Psalm 146:5

Help and Hope

* *

Psalm 84:11

Sun and Shield

* *

ONE OF THESE IS NOT LIKE THE OTHER

Some outline points clearly state what you want to present next in your speech, but something about the way the point sounds doesn't seem to fit, and it is harder to remember. Usually you can solve this problem by making the outline points match—by using the same sentence structure and the same parts of speech. Using a similar construction is called parallelism.

What is the difference in the structure of these three outline points?

I Have A Happier Life If I Am Thankful.

Having a Thankful Heart Precedes Miracles.

God Will Help Grow Thanksgiving in Me

All three outline points are sentences, but the sentences don't match in form or format. I wouldn't be able to remember this outline on stage. I would stumble over the words as I repeated the outline. The audience would have nothing to connect the points. To make a more memorable outline using parallelism, I zeroed in on the phrase A Thankful Heart and changed the outline.

A Thankful Heart is a Happy Heart

A Thankful Heart Precedes Miracles

A Thankful Heart Fills My Life

An outline comprising single words is easy to remember, but these words don't ring true if they are different parts of speech. For example, a presentation on how to keep up with family schedules might have a single-word outline like this:

Clock

Calendar

Coordinate

The outline looks good on the surface. The words seem clear, and all begin with the same letter. On closer inspection, however, we see these words are not the same part of speech. Clock and calendar are nouns. They describe objects. Coordinate is a verb which describes an action. So, the three words are not parallel. The outline can improves by changing the last item to a noun.

Clock

Calendar

Coordination

With this change, the outline flows easily. A speaker could put this three-point outline into his or her mind and stand before a crowd and give a presentation with no notes. The order and grace of the language will stimulate the audience. As an added plus, if you have distractions during your presentation, you as the speaker are not as at risk of forgetting what you planned to say.

The key to a great outline depends on whether you can remember it while on stage.

Once the spotlight shines on you and you see faces in the audience, you will not forget a simple outline. An outline with long, involved sentences is hard to remember. You will probably have to read the outline point—and your audience will not remember it either.

CHAPTER 3
BUILD THE P. I. E. R.

THERE ARE CERTAIN THINGS IN WHICH MEDIOCRITY IS NOT
TO BE ENDURED, SUCH AS POETRY, MUSIC, PAINTING, PUBLIC
SPEAKING." ~ JEAN DE LA BRUYERE

I entered the ballroom where I was to speak to an organization that helped women learn how to interview for a new job. They taught their clients how to prepare effective resumes, how to dress for the interview, and how to answer questions and make the best impression on a potential boss. As I typically do, I arrived early so I could go to the stage and get a feel for the room. That night, the stage was a runway because the group planned a style show. At the back of this beautiful runway, a large podium stood against the wall wedged between a bank of flowers on each side. I stood behind the massive wood lectern and realized I couldn't see most of the audience and they wouldn't be able to see me either since I am short.

At that moment, I knew the best place for me to stand when I spoke to the group was at the end of the runway. I also knew that there was no place for me to put my notes in front of me. I made a decision that I would speak from the end of the runway, and I would do it without my notes. The experience was amazing. Without my notes, I connected to the audience, and my presentation was more animated and spirited than ever before. I had prepared well for the presentation, and I knew my material, but I had never had the courage to walk onto the stage without my iPad in hand. That night was so successful I vowed to put my notes down from that day forward. The experience changed my speaking completely, and I believe it took my abilities to connect with the crowd to new and higher levels. I knew my outline. I knew my illustrations and references, so I gave my talk without the aid of my written prompts. You can do this kind of spur-of-the-moment change if you know your material well and if you have a dynamite outline that allows you to remember what you want to say next, and if you have your opening and closing memorized.

We talked about how creating a pithy outline that you can remember helps you speak without notes but now I'm going to show you the key to fleshing out that outline into a powerful, winsome, wonderful presentation. The tool I use is called P I E R. It is the product of CLASSeminars and Florence Littauer and Marita Tedder, who taught me how to use it and graciously gave me permission to share it with you. This plan has become an intricate part of how I prepare and how I present on stage. If you use this tool, you will speak powerfully—and without notes. You will also be able to adapt your presentation to any timeframe— longer or shorter—without losing the power and effectiveness of the message. Let's discover the P.I.E.R together.

P IS FOR POINT

We have discussed building the points of your outline using sentences or words that you and your audience can remember and grasp. Now I will show you how to make each of those points full-bodied and profound and compelling. Begin by adding the "I" in P I E R.

I is for Instructions

The audience wants to understand how your point applies to them. Instructions or guidelines and directions or challenges show the audience how to implement the point into daily life. When you add instructions to your presentation, you have helped the hearers discover a fresh way to live or think or act. The instruction shows how the point of the message applies to life. When your listeners gain a glimpse of how the point might change their lives, you have a successful presentation.

Instructions give your audience some specific, definable actions. What is the next step each person should take and when and how should he or she take it? Be as detailed and precise as possible as you give these instructions. The instructions may be mental such as a new attitude, or physical such as cleaning out a junk drawer, or spiritual such as reading the Psalms each day, or emotional such as forgiving a past hurt. What activities, arrangements, or deeds will lead to success?

For example, in a presentation about developing a positive attitude, I could instruct the audience to make a list of upbeat statements. I could give them a brief quote to memorize so they will remember to think positively. I might give them a tool to use to help overcome anger—such as counting to ten. I may ask the audience to make a list of 3 people who annoy them and write one positive statement about each of those people each day for a week. All of these are instructions.

E is for Examples

Every presentation must include good illustrations and examples that make the point come alive. The best illustrations and examples are stories. And the best stories are personal stories about you.

It isn't enough for your audience to hear that they need to forgive others unless you show how the act of forgiveness changed relationships and situations in your life.

Stories and illustrations make each concept clearer. Metaphors, word pictures, and stories communicate better than information, advice, or lectures. Personal stories are the best source for illustrations. Dale Carnegie said, "Speakers who talk about what life has taught them never fail to keep the attention of their listeners." Far better than canned or memorized stories, your personal stories will enhance your persona before the crowd. No one can tell your stores like you can tell them. You know the emotions and details intimately. As a bonus, you need not memorize a personal story because you know what happened.

A clever story, an entertaining illustration, or an amusing example keeps your message interesting but should never sidetrack or confuse your audience. Make the point and use an example to support, not distract. Sometimes you must remove extraneous details from the story or portions of the ending so your audience can focus on your main point.

Never tell a story or use an illustration or example unless it makes the point.

I know it is tempting to tell a story because you like the story or you know it will get a laugh, but resist the temptation, only telling the story if it makes your point.

We will work on the structure and building of a great story in chapter 5. But as we consider how to flesh out a point, remember the most important feature of your explanation of each point is a story that illustrates and gives an example of your point.

R is for Reference

Each point needs strength and power. The best way to add heft to your point is to present some authority behind your statements.

Back up and support what you say with facts, data, numbers, statistics, and other measurements or authoritative information. Quotes from respected sources strengthen points. Verses from the Bible and quotations from experts will solidify and reinforce your message. Use all these as ways to give your message credibility.

The Bridge and the P I E R

In chapter one, we learned that our speech has one over-arching point which we have stated in a 15-word (or less) sentence. This sentence is our bridge to the audience. That bridge is then supported by powerful piers—strong sub points—an outline—to support the theme.

And as we learned in chapter two, the outline must be clear, concise, and easily remembered by both the speaker and the audience. Each point in the outline will have a P.I.E.R: Point. Instruction. Example. Reference.

The Beauty of the System

The versatile P.I.E.R. system allows you to speak without notes because you 1) know the Point [outline] 2) know the Instructions, Examples, and References for each point in the outline. And the ultimate beauty of the system is that you can speak for ten minutes or one hour and still present the entire presentation. Here's how: In the PIER system, you will have one point for each outline point, but there may be multiple instructions and a half-dozen examples and many references. If time allows, you give more than one instruction, example, or reference and if the time is short, you give only one of each part of P.I.E.R.

POINT	One Point from the outline
INSTRUCTIONS	As many instructions as fit the topic
EXAMPLE	As many illustrations as fit the topic
REFERENCE	As many verses, statistics, quotes etc. as you can find.

When I coach a client, one of my main goals is to help that speaker build enough confidence to put down his or her notes when they are on stage. The benefits are enormous. First, you will connect with your audience without the barrier of a podium or stand or notebook or iPad. Second, you will respond to how your audience is receiving the information you are giving ... for example, if you note they seem to be a little lost or confused, you can slow down and offer more details. Third, speaking without notes enhances eye contact and personal rapport. Fourth, speaking will become much more fun. Laying down your notes is terrifying—I know. But the benefits are exponential. I hope by the time you finish this book; you will try it.

Chapter 4
Let's Craft a Message

In this chapter, I want to show how to build a presentation from several viewpoints. Whether you use a strict outline or tell a story or use a metaphor or other technique, the crafting of the message is a key to your success.

CAN I BUILD THE ENTIRE MESSAGE AROUND ONE STORY?

Yes, a strong message can be built into and around one central story. If we structure the message around one story, we will still use P.I.E.R. and will follow one of the story structures we discussed in the last chapter.

Let's practice by listing all the facts about one of my stories— when my Great Pyrenees fell into the swimming pool. Here are the basic facts.

- The morning was dusky and foggy as I let Isabelle out the back door. She typically comes back fast because she is afraid of noises and the dark and especially of water. But on this morning, when I opened the door again, she didn't return.

- ☐ Then, I saw her—in the swimming pool.

- ☐ Somehow, she had fallen in and now she was clinging to the side of the pool; her paws digging into the concrete. I ran to her because I know she is terrified of water.

  - ▪ I noticed that her back feet were one inch from some steps, and I tried to get her to swing one foot over just a bit so she could push herself out of the pool.

  - ▪ She wouldn't budge. I considered prying her front paws from the edge of the pool because I know she can swim and could easily paddle to the other steps nearby.

  - ▪ Instead, I took pity on her and reached down and lifted her out of the pool.

Using these basic story facts, I can craft a story that has an opening, a main point, subpoints using P.I.E.R., and a closing.

The Opening

I want to grab my audience's attention. I have this idea that I could talk about Isabelle for a while and not reveal she is a dog. Instead, I will try to make the audience think Isabelle is a person.

I could describe how she hides in the closet when it thunders. I might talk about how a loud noise makes her fearful, for example when a large truck rumbles by. I won't describe Isabelle, but I will speak of her in human terms. Most of the audience will not realize that Isabelle is a dog until I show her photo on the screen.

I know I need to get the audience to buy-in to my premise that Isabelle is a person and is afraid, so I start the presentation with this shocking declaration, "Isabelle is a wuss!"

After I have revealed that Isabelle is a dog, I will weave the story around the foggy morning scene using descriptions of the fog and the semi-darkness. I will use hand gestures to depict how strange to see Isabelle hanging on the side of the pool with her claws, trying to dig into the concrete side of the pool.

THE PRESENTATION

I will tell about the step that is close and the fact that Isabelle can swim and describe how I get Isabelle to take one of those options. Then I will make three points about the incident.

First point: Isabelle was near a step.

Example: If Isabelle would have moved one of her back legs just an inch, she would have been able to get the footing necessary to push herself out of the pool.

Instruction: Sometimes when you are in the worst troubled situation, the answer is nearby. You may need to look around. You too can raise yourself out of the deep waters to safety.

Reference: Hebrews 13:5b "Never will I leave you; never will I forsake you."

Second point: Isabelle knows how to swim.

Example: We taught Isabelle how to swim around the pool until we turned her in the direction of the big steps and the way out of the pool.

Instruction: We may solve our problems by drawing on the skills, expertise, and talents within. All we need to do is calm down and move in the direction of our training to get to safety.

Reference: 1 Corinthians 12:11 "All these are empowered by one and the same Spirit, who apportions to each one individually as he wills."

Third point: On that morning I had mercy on Isabelle.

Example: I reached down, placing my strong arms beneath her front legs and lifted her out.

Instruction: When we are in trouble, God has mercy on us as frail human beings and rescues us from danger.

Reference: "He reached down from on high and took hold of me; he drew me out of deep waters" (Psalm 18:16).

THE CLOSING

When trouble strikes, look around to push yourself out or swim to safety using the skills you have already acquired. Or cry out to God for mercy and He will rescue you. But don't be a wuss!

The structure I used is the normal/conflict/new normal pattern. Normal was Isabelle's typical early morning outdoor foray. Conflict is when she falls in the pool. New normal is when I pull her to safety.

Did you notice how the conflict interrupted the normal? Did you notice the last line in the closing is a repeat of a line in the opening?

****

CAN YOU GIVE ME TIPS IF WE BUILD THE MESSAGE AROUND AN OUTLINE?

Let's build a message using an outline instead of a story. Let's assume our main topic is to be prayer. First, I would do a lot of research on the subject, reading the Bible, finding as many examples of prayer as I could find. I would read books by solid authors—in this case maybe Jennifer Kennedy Dean's *The Praying Life* and Mark Batterson's book, *The Circle Maker*. As I read these, I will find verses and quotes that fit my topic of prayer. I would also go through my personal prayer journal to find nuggets of interesting information and inspiration about prayer. I would listen to my friends as they tell stories about how prayer had brought calm to an otherwise chaotic situation. In all that information, I would choose several important statements about prayer from all this research. I would decide which ideas I want to use and build a memorable outline using one of the different styles. This outline becomes the skeleton of my message. Much of the work needed to put the message together is in the research.

I typically use three separate blank pages to begin the outlining process. (Three assumes I will have 3 points—if there are more or less, use that many pages). On each one of these pages, I write the letters P, I, E, R down the side, writing my outline point next to the P. As I filled in the page with instructions, examples, and references, I will begin forming a powerful message.

MAIN POINT: PRAYER CHANGES LIFE SITUATIONS

Point No 1. _Prayer is Conversation with God_

> Instruction: <u>Treat your prayer time like a daily chat with the heavenly father. Address him directly. He is listening, and he is ready to answer.</u>

Examples: _____

References: _____

Point No 2. Prayer is _____

Instruction: _____

Examples: _____

References: _____

Point No 3. Prayer is _____

Instruction: _____

Examples: _____

References: _____

Notice how stories are fit into the examples section of each point. To be authentic and powerful, these stories should mostly come from my life experience. Craft each story carefully crafted using the techniques you learned in the chapter on story.

CHAPTER 5
STORY IT UP!

"IF YOU DON'T USE STORIES AUDIENCE MEMBERS MAY ENJOY YOUR SPEECH, BUT THERE IS NO CHANCE THEY WILL REMEMBER IT." ~ANDRIL SEDNIEV

The best speaking advice I ever received was three words, "Story it up!" The more stories you add to your illustrations, your overall point, and your sub-points, the more your presentations will reach your audience. Too often I hear speakers who have brilliant points, but they present them to the audience in a list form. Typically, this pattern sounds preachy – full of shoulds and oughts and musts. If your audience hears a story that is an example of the point you want to make, they will remember it.

KEYS TO GREAT STORYTELLING

Key No. 1—An enemy and a hero.

Stories will be bland and dull if there is no fight between good and evil. The concept of enemy vs. hero blossoms everywhere there are good stories. In children's cartoons a good witch battles a bad witch, Elmer Fudd warns Bugs Bunny not to eat the carrots, and the roadrunner is chased by the coyote.

Smart businesses couch the story of the company by hero overcoming the enemy. Agricultural companies fight poor production and now harvest more per acre. Technology companies faced the problem of giant computers that filled the room and were inaccessible to the average person and yet they converted that technological tool to a hand-held device. A food company tells the story of an immigrant who won against the Great Depression by hard work and determination and became the CEO.

Christianity is the ultimate war between good and evil. Sin vs righteousness. Living a full, abundant life vs wasting your life.

Our personal stories can be told with the structure of enemy vs hero. You against a diagnosis. You against a storm. You against yourself or your behaviors such as addictions or poor financial choices. You vs your dreams. You vs your hair! The story of how you overcame your upbringing, dealing with past abuse or neglect.

A story with a struggle will captivate and interest your audience.

Key No. 2—Conflict

Every story needs friction. Otherwise the story will be too sweet or seem too perfect. There should be some obstacles in the way and some struggles to reach the goal. Every bit of suspense and tension in your story makes the story more powerful.

Key No. 3—Surprise

Each story needs at least one surprise. Make the audience think the end of the story is one way, but end it another way. Like pulling a rug out from under them.

Key No. 4—Characters

Use details about the look and style of each character to make the character come alive. Give your characters a certain appearance and a tone of voice. Add some details like hobbies, professions, obsessions, and quirks. If you tell the story with great characters, you will transport the audience to the scene.

When you have these four key ingredients to your story, you will need to develop some story telling techniques.

TELL ME A STORY

Tell the story as an organic part of your point. Speak conversationally—not too perfect. Not like a corporate officer giving a report or like mother goose talking to children. Use the sound of your voice to create a bond between you and your audience. Be authentic and personal. It's your story; tell it like only you can tell it.

1)   **Use dialogue.**

Tell the story as interaction between your characters. Use a deep voice for one character and high tinny voice for another character. Your audience will follow the story by knowing which character is saying what. Change positions on the stage for one character (facing right) and the other character (facing left). If one character is bigger than the other, raise your shoulders when you speak for the big character and fold your shoulders in and bend your knees when speaking for the smaller character.

Dialogue shouldn't be in complete sentences. Listen to how people around you talk and adapt your story dialogue to match styles and language. People talk in phrases, not sentences. One character might say, "yep" instead of "yes" and one character might miss pronounce a word which can produce humorous exchange.

2)   *Show don't tell.*

Telling is saying words that communicate what the audience should think or what you want them to feel. Showing is expressing the idea with description that helps the audience "see" the scene or person. Instead of saying a character is introverted, describe how shy she acts—hiding behind a tree or crouching behind a table. Instead of telling that a character is tall, either stand as tall as you can stand or say the character has to duck through doors. Slam your fist on a table instead of saying a character is angry. Pull your collar up tight if it is cold or give an exaggerated yawn if the character is tired.

3)   *Repetition*

Repeating a word or phrase or characteristic is a creative technique to make the story more interesting. I watched the speech that won the national championship and loved how the speaker used a repetitious sentence. When he was young, his grandmother said, "I see something in you, but I don't know what it is." Throughout his story, various people influenced him and each one said the same line, "I see something in you, but I don't know what it is." At the end, he was ready to challenge the audience. He looked the audience over and said, "I see something in you, but I don't know what it is." The repetition made his story compelling. He won the national championship.

I use a story in one of my presentations that describes a certain highway in Texas. I traveled up Highway 45 and turned right on Highway 79. Then I tell how my daughter, my son-in-law, and my husband each traveled up these two highways. Then I tell the audience, "About that time, Hurricane Ike came ashore and traveled up Highway 45 and turned right on Highway 79." I could have said it felt as if the storm followed us as we tried to get out of its path, but using this repetitious pattern makes the audience live the story with me.

4)   *Accents.*

I challenge you to experiment with various kinds of accents to use in the dialogue in your stories. Practice and then only use the good ones. I've worked on all kinds of accents to help tell my stories. I'm not very good at it, but I've developed a few phrases I can use. I tell a story of being in an English church, and I've practiced speaking in a British accent like all the people in the story. However, I only use one sentence from one person because I'm not very good at accents. I've worked and worked on that one particular sentence. I am careful to tell the story in such a way that no one else speaks directly until I'm ready with the accent. The addition of the flavor of the different cadences and stages of the accent add a lot of fun to the story. One caution is to be sure you are not belittling or smearing any people group with your fake accent. Better to leave it out than to offend.

Does the Story Make Your Point?

Does the story you are using make the point of your message? If not, file it away for another time. An editor once told me, "Karen, the only reason you have that story in that chapter is because you like the story." The editor was right. I really liked that story, but I realized the story didn't reinforce or illustrate my point. If the story doesn't make the point, then leave it out.

Ask, "Does this story make the point?"

Some stories could make several points. During that hurricane when my family and I evacuated has given me numerous adventures to use as part of my presentations. Whichever hurricane story I use always relates to the message/point of that presentation. If I'm speaking on fear or facing storms, I use one part of the hurricane story. If I'm speaking on personal perspective, another part of those hurricane stories will be more effective.

Stories are irresistible. Stories teach truth. Examples get to the point quicker. Stories get the job done better than facts or finger pointing or statistics or sales pitches. A well-told story reaches deep into the hearer's heart. Your story should lead to their story.

NO ONE CARES ABOUT YOUR RESUME, BUT THEY WILL LOVE YOUR STORY! ~UNKNOWN

The best stories or illustrations come from your life. These life stories teach truth. Be alert to everything around you; examples to get your point across are everywhere.

"STORYTELLING IS THE MOST POWERFUL WAY TO PUT IDEAS INTO THE WORLD." – ROBERT MCKEE

STORIES NEED PLOT

Examine your story to determine if it fits one of the basic plots of storytelling. There are at least seven.

1) Overcoming the Monster – Red Riding Hood or Jurassic Park
2) Rags to Riches – The Karate Kid or Jane Eyre or Cinderella or My Fair Lady
3) Quest for a Treasure – Moby Dick or Lord of the Rings or Raiders of the Lost Ark
4) Voyage of Hero Who comes Back a Changed Person – Back to the Future or The Lion, the Witch, and the Wardrobe or Toy Story

5) Comedy (happy ending) – Pride and Prejudice or Four Weddings and a Funeral
6) Tragedy (events go wrong) – Anna Karenina or Romeo and Juliet or Bonnie and Clyde
7) Rebirth/Escape from Death – Jonah or A Christmas Carol or Sleeping Beauty

Stories Need Structure

If you are a novelist or a fan of novels, you probably know that stories have structure and follow a pattern. As you develop how to tell your stories on stage, you should also fit the story into a proven structure. Let's look at a few of these patterns.

Using the structure of 1) beginning 2) middle 3) end provides a framework on which to hang your story, and it gives you a sequence of events—a progression. But it doesn't help build tension or show conflict or provide intrigue to the story.

One of my favorite structures is a simplified version of the story arc.

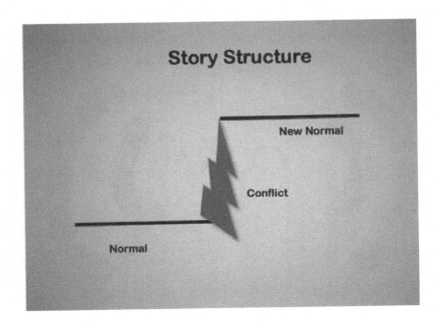

Show the audience what is normal. Then disrupt the normal with a conflict. Then resolve the conflict and show a new normal.

Normal can be good. A story might depict a man with a good job and a happy family. Then he loses his job and his house burns down and one of his children gets arrested. The story follows all these conflicts until finally the man gets a better job and builds a new house and his child comes home for a happy reunion.

Normal can be bad. A story might depict a girl living in an abusive or dysfunctional home. It's not a pretty picture, but it is her normal. The conflict might be how a relative helps her escape the abuse and brings her to a safe home situation. Conflict doesn't have to be bad, but it is disruptive. And in this scenario, the new normal might be when the girl forgives her abusive parent.

Without the normal, no one can understand the trauma of the conflict. A story without conflict is bland and probably boring.

****

Another story structure type is nested loops. In this framework, the story asks three questions: Why? What? and How?

In this pattern, you describe the "why" of an insight or a significant idea by surrounding it with what happened and how it happened. The nested loop pattern invites the audience into the deepest part of your story and your identity.

You might tell a story about your experience of backpacking across Europe before college. The details of how you lived and what you saw could show why you attended the University you chose or the major you declared.

Your story might be about finding your life's purpose and commitment. The steps you took, the methods you tried, the struggle you experienced would all be part of the loops around your quest.

The center of the nested loops structure is your core message, and you add other stories around it to explain what happened and how you came to the central theme.

★ ★ ★ ★ ★ ★ ★ ★ ★ ★ ★ ★ ★ ★

A third story structure is comparison and contrast. In this structure, the real-world story is told alongside a better-world ideal story. Occasionally these two worlds collide. The comparison / contrast is between what is and what could be.

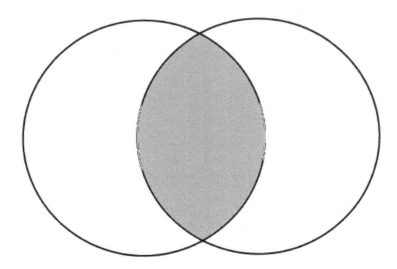

The story of life difficulties can be contrasted and compared to a trouble-free life of ease.

The story of your quest to find peace with God can be contrasted and compared to the good and bad that happens to you.

The story of a marriage filled with fighting and conflict would intersect with times of tranquility and peace and even joy.

Contrast and comparison causes the audience to desire the better situation and creates hope.

★ ★ ★ ★ ★ ★ ★ ★ ★ ★ ★ ★ ★ ★

Another story structure that works for many stories is known by the Latin phrase In Medias Res, which means in the middle. The story begins and then flashes back to the backstory of how the event happened. You see this technique in movies, which begin with a spectacular moment such as a car wreck or a burning building and then these words flash on the screen: "Three Years Earlier."

BEGINNING	MIDDLE	END

▶ START HERE

This method grabs attention quickly and causes the audience to want to hear the end of the story. Be careful about telling backstory for too long. Audiences get frustrated and impatient and want to get back to the action and the final resolution of the story.

I saw a video of a speaker who began his speech telling an emotional story about a man who murdered a Rabbi and planned the bombing of the World Trade Center. Then speaker said, "That man was my father." His presentation was about his childhood and how he eventually rejected his father's path for the path of peace. He managed the backstory with careful descriptions and emotions.

* * * * * * * * * * * * * *

Another method for building your presentation is Hitting the Brick Wall, often called the False Start structure.

The story begins and something gets in the way or disrupts the expectations. The brick wall is a surprise, which keeps your audience's attention. The character in the story must recover from the shock of the brick wall and find a new way to achieve his goal.

An athlete is number one on the stats and has a career ending injury. He must find a new way to live without being the best at his sport.

A Christ follower gets arrested and convicted for a crime she didn't commit. But she lives her new normal in prison by telling others about the Gospel.

The false start method allows you to help the audience see solutions to problems as they watch the story unfold.

Underlying Truth and Genuineness

Sometimes a story fails because it is missing the underlying truth or motivation in the resolution—the why. Award-winning author and my friend, Tricia Goyer, wrote about what makes a good story using as her example the book and movie *Unbroken*.

"I love WWII. I loved the book, and I wanted to love the movie. I liked the movie, but something was missing. What the book had that the movie missed was the "why" of Louie's story. How was he able to stay strong? Why did he not surrender? The book shows how God used important people in his life who believed in him. Also, it shows how after the war Louie was broken. He surrendered ... to God, and God healed all the broken pieces.

Anyone can take the "highlights" of someone's life (good and bad) and string them into a "story," but the key to every story is the "why." It is the heart-message that resonates with all of us.

During a moment where Louie faced certain death, he cried out to God and said that if God saved Him, then he would follow God with his life.

God took Louie up on that. God carried Louie through the darkest nights, and when Louie got to the end of himself, and truly surrendered, then God took all those broken pieces and used him to share with multitudes that true strength and healing comes from God alone.

Could this have been added in the movie? Yes. It would have taken some subtle moments to share the internal faith story, and it would have changed the movie for me and for other viewers."

Common Blunders in Storytelling and How to Fix Them

Long Set-Up instead of Getting to the Story

FIX:

- [ ] Trim the backstory-set up. Leave out history or details that aren't necessary.

- [ ] Get to the point without rambling

Observation instead of In-the-Scene

FIX:

- [ ] Put the audience in the car using descriptions of the bumpy ride or the terror of speed.

- [ ] Let them walk into the airport with you by showing what they see and hear and smell.

- [ ] Use phrases such as "Imagine if …" "Ride with me as I …" If you were with me, you…"

- [ ] Have you been in a football stadium on a hot day? That's where I was when…"

Speed instead of Pauses

FIX:

- [ ] Use facial expression and body language of the characters to convey emotion or anger or surprise.

- [ ] Allow the audience to read between the lines by slowing down the conversation and/or stopping to react to the dialogue.

- [ ] Show the feeling before you say it … Sigh to show disgust or frustration before you say the words. Raise a hand before asking the question.

Narration instead of Dialogue.

FIX:

- [ ] Get to the dialogue fast.

- [ ] Speak the dialogue in present tense (in the scene-not in the past).

- [ ] Allow the dialogue to set up the conflict.

"NARRATION IS RE-TELLING.
DIALOGUE IS RE-LIVING." ~
ANONYMOUS

Long instead of Short

FIX:

- [ ] Remove unnecessary details and descriptions. If the story is about 4 days of activity, condense it to one day by combining the action.

- [ ] Try to condense the story to one line or three lines of dialogue.

- [ ] Build a composite person instead of a large group of people.

PRUNE YOUR STORIES

Too often we tell our stories using every detail and over explaining each part of the story. If we tell every detail, the story will take over the presentation, and we will lose the opportunity to make the point and help our audience find solutions to their problems. No story is that important. I had a major role in a large corporation for more than 30 years until the dynamics of the company took a different turn after a foreign entity purchased the business. I lost my job as did numerous others. I could tell that story for days because I know every detail of what happened, but you would be bored. I have crafted that story, cutting details and unnecessary information so that I can tell the story in about six minutes, which fits into a 30-40 minute presentation. Once I spoke for five minutes. I wanted to use this story, so I cut out every extraneous detail and cut the story to ninety seconds. Combined with my outline, the story fit well into my five-minute talk.

Learn to tell your stories shorter by cutting the details. Here are some areas you could cut.

1) Dates/days/time – does it really matter what day the story happened?
2) Why you were at that place at that time?—does this detail impact the story?
3) Details of your personality type and how you reacted—would one or two words explain it?
4) Chronological details—get to the point of the story even if you have to rearrange how it happened.
5) Choose emotions over information—your feelings and your emotional state are better than straight facts
6) Find the punch line—develop a perfect pithy, concise punch line conveying the emotion, the point, the challenge.

Stories are better than facts, or statistics, or logic, or even sales pitches. Think about the commercials that you remember above all the others. They almost always have a story woven in. Top marketers know that they must tell a story if they are going to have successful sales. They know this because they know that people react and respond to story. You need to understand this principle and use story as much as possible in your presentation.

Think of some commercials that tell a story—the little boy who thinks he is Darth Vader, the horse who misses the little dog; the family who finds the perfect insurance. These stories follow the patterns and structure we have learned in this book and make the point of the commercial with a poignant or funny punch line. The producers prepare a 90-second version, which is the full story, and after it has aired for a while, they will also air the 60-second and 30-second versions. The story is the same, but in an abbreviated form. Sometimes we don't have time for all the details.

As you prepare your stories and illustrations, ask yourself, "Can I tell it short?"

BECOMING A GREAT STORYTELLER

Every story must make a point. Never tell a story just because it is funny or cute or because you like it. If the story doesn't make the point, file it away for another time. When you use a personal story or illustration, you will lead the audience to their story. The connection between your story and theirs is critical to the success of your illustration.

Stories are important because they make hearers apply the deeper message of the presentation. Story is the chief way you capture the heart of your audience. Story makes the point stick and the action achievable.

Our brains are wired to hear and respond to story – not bullet points.

It is rare for a hearer to remember the points of a presentation, but the same person will store away all the truth in a story and will make a personal connection.

Use true stories and illustrations. Audiences recognize fiction quickly. If I hear a speaker tell a joke using the names of people in the audience, I erect a wall because I know this speaker isn't always honest. When a speaker uses a story copied from social media or found in one of the many emails that flood our inboxes, the audience thinks the speaker has done little research and is probably shallow and uninteresting. Some in the audience will have seen the social media post or have received the email too. Don't risk using random stories and illustrations in your presentation. Instead, use your amazing true stories.

CHAPTER 6
WHERE ARE ALL THE STORIES FOUND?

O nce you recognize ideas for talks and examples or stories, then record those examples and stories so you can retrieve them later. Don't rely on your memory, no matter how good it is. Keep a pen and small notebook or index cards handy. Go nowhere without a way to record the examples you'll see. Since most of us carry our phone everywhere, put them in an app for lists or record them digitally on the spot. As you write the example, do a messy brain dump or knowledge transfer, simply recording the details. Don't judge the material and don't try to add humor. Your job is to put enough in writing, so you won't forget the incident. You will massage and flesh it out later.

Watch for stories wherever you are every day. Be alert all day, every day. I have an "Idea List" in my phone and duplicated in Evernote,[a] and I place every story on that list—some I've used before and some I haven't used in a speech yet. For example, I have archived a story of being in a hospital waiting room. In that drab gray room, I observed all the people and kept some notes, Later, I built a story about waiting around that scene. But I've never used that story in a presentation–yet.

If you are at a public event, notice the crowd around you. What are people doing? One time I was at a football game and saw a man who was apparently so disgusted with the team and the coach that after every play he raised his hands and flipped his palms outward, saying, "Whatever!" It became comical to watch.

No matter what play the coach called or how the team executed it, the man was never impressed. He just shrugged them off, saying, "Whatever." I wrote this brief story in my notebook. While I haven't figured out how to use it yet, except right here, I am sure the story will be a perfect illustration someday.

You can find stories in everything that happens to you. My friend Ken Davis was on a plane ready for takeoff when the airport crews delayed the flight to clean bugs off the wings. He found the humor in the details and then turned the story into a message about clearing the bugs out of our life. If he can build an entertaining yet powerful message from bugs on a plane, you can find examples in your life too.

Keep a small notebook in your pocket or purse, so you can record the funny and interesting happenings around you. Also, keep a pad of paper and pen by your bedside for those thoughts that flash through your mind during the night. I know it's not fun to turn on the light or get your glasses so you can write your thoughts, but if you don't, you will be even more annoyed when morning comes and you remember you had a wonderful idea during the night but can't recall what it is. You will never remember all the observations during the day or the good ideas you get during the night unless you record the idea.

If I get a good thought during the night or while I'm busy with something else, I usually write a few words of description. I write just enough so I'll remember the story. When morning comes or I have a free moment, then I record the essence of the story. When I get ready to use that story in a presentation, I will flesh out the details from my memory.

STORIES FROM YOUR PERSONAL LIFE

Your life makes the best illustrations because you know the stories that happen to you. Consider your past and your present, and you will discover many outstanding examples. By answering the following questions, you can discover how your life is a treasure chest of examples.

1) Where were you born? How did this location affect your values and beliefs?

2) Name and describe your brothers and sisters?

3) Did your family live in the city or country? What stories remind you of the house or apartment?

4) What decade were you born in, and what was happening in the world?

5) Describe your elementary and high school experiences. What stories do you remember from those days?

6) Describe your friends. Could one of these friends or a composite of several friends become a character in a story?

7) What did you do for fun as a kid? Is there some humorous or touching activity that will create a response in your audience?

8) What did your parents, teachers, and other adults in your life expect of you as a child? (Be seen not heard. Make good grades. Excel at sports. Work in the family business.) Does one of these expectations bring a story to mind that you could tell your audience to make a point?

9) What factors contributed to the happiness or sadness of your childhood? Consider your weight issues, financial situation, neighborhood, friends or lack of friends, or family dynamics. How could telling one of those stories create a rapport between you and your audience?

10) How did you cope with unpleasant situations as a child? As a teen? Knowing this defense mechanism about yourself might be important for your audience to know.

11) List some of your favorite activities as a child and as a teen.

These sometimes-silly memories can insert humor and fun into your presentations.

12) Do you have expertise in any of the following areas? If so, these might be great topics for you to pursue as you develop presentations.

- ☐ Music
- ☐ Health
- ☐ Family relationships
- ☐ Job hunting
- ☐ Writing
- ☐ Poetry
- ☐ Sports
- ☐ Outdoor activities
- ☐ Dance

Your past is like a notebook full of illustrations from your personal story. Your present is a window, revealing examples and anecdotes. Your future is a doorway to rich stories that will enhance and illustrate future presentations.

As you build your list of story ideas or presentation ideas, consider your life and where you might look for inspiration.

Consider Hidden Stories. You may not want to remember some of the most powerful stories if it requires you to think of a hard place in your life. For example, when I think about the last few years of my mother's life, I feel guilty because I could not help her when she became confused. I loved her so much and she was a terrific mother, but I was ill-equipped to handle her last days well. Another kind of hidden story would be when you have caused someone else pain. Perhaps you've said something you shouldn't have said, or you failed to be loyal when a friend needed you. Telling that story to your audience will show authenticity and humility. Be sure the story makes the point.

Consider Family Stories. If your family is like mine when we get together, we remember events and people and we tell the same stories over and over. Some of these stories will work wonderfully in your presentations if they make the point well.

Consider Funny Stories. If something makes you laugh, it will probably make your audience laugh too. For example, my friend Carolyn told me about how her twins nearly drove her crazy with their energy and never-ending questions. Like most mommas, one day she couldn't cope, so she threw herself across the bed. One twin said, "Momma, is there anything you can think of that you like about us?" I howl every time I hear that story so I know it will work in a presentation.

Consider Painful Stories. If you've been hurt by another person (and who hasn't), the story of how you dealt with the pain might be a great illustration in your next presentation.

Consider Life-Changing Stories. I was part of a leadership team of women who led a large community Bible study group. In those early Saturday morning team meetings, I observed how women from all walks of life handled personal situations and big questions. I have never been the same. I've used variations of that story in numerous presentations as I've talked about commitment, honesty, and devotion.

Consider Loser Stories. When I lost my job after 33 years of being a rising corporate star, my world imploded. But now I believe this horrific event challenged and changed me into a person with a better set of purposes in life. Audiences respond to my difficult situation by remembering their personal loser situations.

Consider Winner Stories. While embarrassing stories may show our vulnerability, stories of our victories inspire audiences too.

Can the Audience Relate?

When you use an example that relates to the audience, it will be powerful, memorable, and meaningful. It will reaffirm the point you are trying to make. When you go into a city to speak, do some research and understand the locale. Know about the local baseball team or that the city's basketball team is in the playoffs. Your audience will love you for knowing their world.

As you decide what illustrations to use, keep your audience in mind. Use what is familiar to them to make your points. Think about what they likely will know and not know. Remember the infamous faux pas by a national politician who said farmers didn't need the Internet. He wasn't up to date on farming techniques, which include tractors with computers and Wi-Fi to help the farm worker prepare, plant, and harvest the fields. He didn't understand his audience or their needs.

Who is in your audience—accountants, pastors, salespeople, moms, grandmothers, insurance executives, Bible study teachers, bankers, women only, men only?

The Bible tells about how Paul and Barnabus understood their audience. The two men were in Lystra. Paul had healed a lame man, and the crowds went wild, saying the men were gods come down to earth. They thought Paul and Barnabus were reincarnations of Zeus and Hermes. The men quieted the crowd, saying, "we are humans not gods." Paul preached to them about the one true God.

When he was speaking in another town, Paul began his message with a Jewish history lesson because he knew this was a Jewish crowd. In fact, he started with creation. In each case, his starting point was different because he knew the crowd.

Information touches the mind and brain. Story touches the emotion. When you touch the spirit, you have helped your audience experience the emotion—such as joy, hope, peace, faith. If you reach your audience through facts and stories, you will be a part of lives that will transform. Your audience will find new courage and uncover values that matter.

Appropriate

Not only should your stories make the point of your message, your illustrations should be appropriate and relevant. If you tell how God changed your life 20 years ago and don't tell how He touched your life this week, your illustration will feel tired. If you only tell how God intervened in your life years ago, the audience will wonder, "What has God done for you lately?" Tell old stories if they make the point, but add current, fresh illustrations, too.

Chapter 7
Grab Them from the Beginning

"THE FIRST 30 SECONDS AND THE LAST 30 SECONDS HAVE THE
MOST IMPACT IN A PRESENTATION." ~PATRICIA FRIPP

Within the first few seconds, the audience will decide if they like you and whether they think you have something to say. They will either sit on the edge of their seats in anticipation or lean back, fold their arms, and expect to be bored.

Never use those first precious few seconds in a frivolous way.

If you use the opening to apologize ("I'm not really a speaker…"), then you will never gain the trust of the audience. If you talk about the weather ("Isn't this cold in May crazy!"), then the audience will perceive you as bland. If you begin by thanking the event planner and team and commenting on the decorations ("Isn't it fun to see all the different tables?"), the audience will assume you are going to bore them with the obvious throughout the presentation. You can thank the event planner during the presentation, even the second paragraph of your speech, but never use those valuable first seconds for polite talk.

Begin immediately with a powerful, brief, clear, interesting opening to capture the audience's attention. Hearers will snap to attention and engage with you from the first minute. Start with passion.

A Fuse

A great opening is like a fuse that gets your audience fired up. The opening is the only chance you have to make your audience want to hear your presentation. Make it memorable. The difference between a great opening and a lifeless one is like the difference between the excitement of saying, "Once upon a time ..." and the boredom of, "Now open your book to page ten just like we did last week." Your audience will either feel excitement to hear what you have to say, or they will begin fidgeting in their seats and checking their cell phones.

Establish Need

Why are you there to speak? Why should the audience listen? Is there a problem to overcome? Is there a solution you have discovered? Are you an expert that has information they want? Your opening line shows them how you are going to inform, inspire, or challenge them throughout your speech.

Opening Tools

The Promise

Show the audience how you will help them through whatever problem you've introduced in your opening. Imagine if you had begun your presentation by saying, "The building is on fire!" You would have the audience's attention and they would be frightened and ready to panic. They would look to you for direction. But you don't want to leave them hanging. Immediately, you would say, "I'll show you four ways to get out of the building."

If your powerful opening line startles listeners, they will pay attention. Then quickly promise how you will help them, how you will meet their need. For example, many people desire to have a quiet time of meditation in the morning, but day after day they don't have enough time or find some other excuse not to do it. What if you said, "If you listen to me for the next 30 minutes, I will guarantee you a consistent and powerful quiet time each morning." Use a line such as, "You are going to receive ..." or "You will walk out of this building with the tools for ..."

A good way to determine if you are making a good promise is to ask yourself: "Who cares?"

The Imagination

Transport your audience to a time and space and make them feel the emotion. Ric Elias begins one of his presentations this way, "Imagine a plane at 3000 feet suddenly filling with smoke and the engines making a clack-clack sound. I had a unique seat that day. I was sitting in seat 1D."

The key to making the audience feel is the detail in your statement. What descriptions will help them feel they are there with you?

Begin with a scenario: "Picture this: _____." Fill in the blank from what you know about the audience. If they are salespeople, "Picture this: You have won the Best Salesperson Award!" Or "Picture this: You didn't have a single profitable sale last quarter." If the audience is a group of moms, "Picture this: Your toddlers pried open a paint can and somehow splattered bright red splotches on the floors and ceilings of your living room." Then make a promise. Today I'll show you how to react.

Another imagination tool is asking, "What if..." Your audience will follow your logic and come to good conclusions if you allow them into your process. What if we always told the truth—no matter what? Then offer some good reasons to tell the full truth—integrity, understanding, less confusion. Then offer some situations why telling the whole truth may not be the best course—hurting someone's feelings, causing pain. The audience will follow and expect some guidelines and insight into truthfulness.

Quiet Pause

For 3-5 seconds look at the crowd and don't make a sound. Let them settle into putting their focus on you. If you do this maneuver, your opening line must be strong or funny or both.

Statistics

Statistics are a great opening when you state them powerfully in a way that the audience instantly grabs the meaning. When using statistics, be intentional about how you present them. Instead of listing the statistics, interpret them. What does the statistic mean to the audience? Don't say the numbers in confusing ways: "Out of 3,765 people surveyed, 1,028 answered. Of those 1,028 who responded, 924 said they..." Some in your audience will try to do the math and will miss whatever you say next. Instead of using numbers, make the point powerful by giving the analysis. "One-third of the population will..." If you can involve the audience, they will remember the statistic, "Look at your neighbor – one of you won't be back next year. Fifty percent of people don't renew membership."

"One in three people will develop lung disease."

"More than half of the people in this room will face divorce or separation in marriage."

"Only 1 percent of teenage girls desire to become a homemaker."

If you can add humor to the statistic, it will become even more powerful. An older man gave the statistic that 79 percent of single adults live together before getting married. Then he said, "Back in my day, we called it 'shacking up!'" He countered the dismal statistic with the humor, but those of us who heard him speak never forgot the statistic.

Adding humor helps a statistic stick. Did you know the number one fear most people have is public speaking? In a survey, 41 percent of people named it as their number one fear. In that same survey, only 19 percent listed death as their number one fear. Jerry Seinfeld said, "That means at a funeral, the person giving the eulogy would rather be in the casket!"

Use stats within a story. In a battle between story and stats, story would win every time. So use stats in a creative and interesting way.

Make a Shocking Statement

As soon as you reach the center of the stage, say something that surprises your audience. A pastor came to the stage, took a long look at the crowd, and shouted, "What in the world is wrong with you?" He let the words sink in and then said, "Those are the words my wife said to me this week when I…" Then he built a message around the story.

Remember the story of my Great Pyrenees? The beginning sentence for this presentation is: "Isabelle is a wuss!" I tell how scared Isabelle is of loud noises and sudden movements. Later in the story, the audience learns that Isabelle is a dog. The story of her falling into the swimming pool is the basis for a three-point message on trusting God. My opening sentence works because my audience assumes Isabelle is a person, and they are shocked that I would publicly label someone in such an unkind way.

Ask Questions

A question is a great tool for opening lines. It engages the audience and gets everyone focused on the subject.

"How many of you are grandmothers? Who knew it would be such a glorious experience! It's your reward for not killing your children!"

"How many of you ate out at a restaurant last week?"

"Who is from another state?"

When asking a question of your audience, raise your hand as if you were about to answer the question, and lean toward the audience. This will signal to them (1) that you are about to ask a question; and (2) that they should respond by raising their hands.

When asking a question, you will naturally eliminate a certain percentage of your audience who can't answer the question yes or no. So it is important to follow the question with a statement that includes the rest of the audience.

"How many of you are mothers?" After the response, ask, "How many of you had a mother?"

"Who in the audience is from Texas?" After the response, ask, "Who of you got here as fast as you could?"

Story

Beginning your presentation with a well-told story will engage and captivate your audience. Be sure that the story fits your message and that the point in the story is part of your message. A story at the beginning is not a rapport builder – unless it powerfully fits into your bridge. When you tell the story, use descriptive, colorful, emotional words.

When coaching a group about living excellently, I begin with this story:

> I once tried a new cheesecake recipe. The ingredients were expensive – several kinds of imported cheeses, special cream, and twelve eggs. I began mixing it all together, and as I dropped in the last egg, I noticed that it didn't quite look right. Have you ever seen a "pretty good" egg? Something about the color and the look of it seemed a little off. But then I thought about all the expensive ingredients were already in the mixture, and I needed that cheesecake for a party, so I stirred the egg in. But I couldn't serve it at the party. I had to buy a cake to serve because I knew about the less-than-excellent egg.

After telling the story, I challenge my audience to reach for excellence (and I can't resist calling it "egg-cellence" at least once during the presentation), to always continue learning, and to never settle for second best. The opening story is the catalyst for the points.

Quote

A quotation can be a powerful hook to grab your audience's attention, especially when you use your voice to add drama and pathos.

When I am teaching speaking techniques live to clients, I often start with this Robert Frost quote, "Half the world is composed of people who have something to say and can't, and the other half of people who have nothing to say and keep on saying it."

My friend Lael Arrington speaks about living large and squeezing all the best out of life. She often begins her presentation with a C. S. Lewis quote.

"We are half-hearted creatures, fooling about with drink and sex and ambition like an ignorant child who wants to go on making mud pies in a slum because he cannot imagine what is meant by the offer of a holiday at the sea."

Her audiences are intrigued by this powerful quote and the stunning way she quotes it.

* * * * * * * * * * * * * * *

Brainstorm how you might use one of the following quotes as a beginning to a presentation.

"Be yourself; everyone else is already taken." ~Oscar Wilde

"A person may think their own ways are right, but the Lord weighs the heart" (Proverbs 21:2).

"A friend is someone who knows all about you and still loves you." ~Elbert Hubbard

"A woman is like a tea bag; you never know how strong it is until it's in hot water." ~Eleanor Roosevelt

"I have not failed. I've just found 10,000 ways that won't work." ~Thomas A. Edison

"If you judge people, you have no time to love them." ~Mother Teresa

"A bird doesn't sing because it has an answer, it sings because it has a song." ~Maya Angelou

"A fool finds pleasure in wicked schemes, but a person of understanding delights in wisdom" (Proverbs 10:23).

Use Drama

A dramatic beginning will captivate your audience. Consider the difference between introducing your topic by saying, "I'm going to talk to you today about security in schools," or by saying,

> "Tobacco." (long pause)

> "Alcohol." (long pause)

> "Guns." (long pause)

>> "These are the items seized in a sixth-grade locker inspection at the junior high in your town yesterday."

This more dramatic introduction (which Andrew Dlugan uses) will grab the audience's attention much better.

Jane Goodall, the naturalist, opened all her presentations with a loud chimp scream. What could be more dramatic or riveting?

Work on your opening more than the rest of your presentation. Use strong verbs, and a tight sentence structure. Make it powerful. If you begin with a story, then be sure it is an engaging story with a powerful point. Study story structure to be sure you have all the elements of a good story in yours.

I never recommend that you memorize your speech, but I highly encourage you to memorize your opening

The opening is not another speech. One pastor spends so much time on setting up the history behind his sermon that he then must rush through his points. Time yourself. The opening is to set the presentation up. Present a problem and tell them how you are going to help solve it.

Never tell jokes to open your presentation. These three words are a hard rule because your audience has probably already heard the joke and you probably can't tell it well either. Comedians train for years to develop the skills such as wordplay, inflection, and timing to tell a joke well. Unless you have been thoroughly trained, stay away from jokes. And just to be clear, never tell a joke by inserting actual people's names into the joke as if it really happened. More than half your audience will already know the joke, and you will lose credibility with them by telling it as if it is a true story.

The opening should introduce the topic, the problem you are going to help the audience solve, or the truth you will teach. A great opening overcomes stage fright. If you use a story or quote opening, then be sure it has a point and that the point is made clearly. The opening must draw your audience to you. Grab them from the first word, and they will stay with you to the end.

Memorize your opening. Use strong verbs and a tight sentence structure. Make it powerful. Practice your opening. Stand up and speak the whole opening aloud.

Make them sit on the edge of their seats, not settle back and expect to be bored.

CHAPTER 8
THE BIG FINALE

"EVERY STORY HAS AN ENDING. BUT IN LIFE, EVERY ENDING IS
A NEW BEGINNING." ~UNKNOWN

In the same way the opening draws the audience in, connects them with you, and launches the audience into your world, the closing is a summary, a review, an opportunity to stress the importance of your points, and it often calls for a commitment or presents a challenge. The closing will leave the audience satisfied.

Use a powerful sentence to bring the message to the ultimate climax. Construct the sentence with strong verbs and description. Add a challenge to commitment or action. Make the closing line upbeat and leave them with renewed enthusiasm.

SUM IT UP

In my presentations about women's friendships, I speak about how the luscious qualities of chocolate compare to the luscious qualities of friendship. My last line is, "So from now on, let chocolate be your cue for great friendships." This statement wraps up the discussion about how forgiveness is as luxurious as Godiva chocolate or how loyalty is like a meringue on a chocolate pie (it covers everything).

At the end of my presentation titled, "If You Give A Girl A Giant," I say, "Let's go kill a giant today!"

At the end of my presentation built on Isabelle being a wuss, I say, "Don't be a wuss!"

At the end of my presentation titled, "Why Can't You Be Normal Like Me?", my last line is, "Different is not wrong … it's just different."

Throughout the presentation, I know exactly what my closing line is going to be, so I never stumble to wrap things up.

CLOSING STYLES

Repeat the Outline

A great way to end the presentation is to repeat the points of the outline and summarize or challenge your audience with the changes you want them to make. If you have used action points in the message, then repeat them. "Today, do this. Tomorrow, do this." If your outline is sentences or verbs, repeat the outline and add a closing challenge.

"God answers personal, peaceful, persistent prayers. Will you pray today?"

"We've seen how God is able, available, and anxious to help us in troubled times. What will you do the next time you face a problem?"

Use a Poem or Quote or Prayer

A poem that fits the message of your presentation will evoke an emotional response from your hearers, as long as you speak it well using proper inflection in your voice. A well-crafted quote will help the audience see your point in one more way. A funny poem fills your audience with laughter and happy thoughts as they leave your presentation.

If you want to pray at the end, use this sentence, "I'd like to pray for you, and then I have one more thing to tell you." Using this sentence like this will prevent an awkward moment at the end of your prayer when the audience doesn't know if you are finished and whether they should applaud. You tell them something is coming after the prayer, then you pray. Then you make your last statement before leaving the stage. Ending in this way helps the audience feel the ending in case they want to applaud and eliminates any awkward moments after the prayer. This method is also a signal to the event planner that your presentation is finished.

MEMORIZE YOUR CLOSING

Whatever you intend to do at the end should be so clear in your mind that you can go there from any point in your message. You never know what might happen while you are speaking. Some technical disaster, some emergency, or some other interruption might get you off your outline and the points you intended to cover. But if you know your ending, nothing can get you so distracted that you will forget how to end.

- Know your beginning line and you'll always be able to start, even if the size of the crowd or the bright lights make you nervous.

- Know your ending lines and you can always get to the end no matter what happens during the presentation, or what you may have had to leave out in the middle of it.

If your ending repeats a line or comment from your opening, your presentation will make a complete circle. Repeat the question you started your presentation with or refer to the story or the statistic from the beginning. Great closings change everything.

USE A FINAL STORY

I was thrilled to discover a pastor we had known many years ago was to speak at an event where I would be. I loved this man and his preaching for many years. When we arrived at the venue, I was surprised to see how much he had aged. Funny how we never think we have aged but notice it in others. I wondered if the pastor would still have the same fire and vigor and dynamic delivery of his younger years. I didn't need to worry because even though he was not as steady on his feet as when he was younger, when he stepped to the podium, he was incredible. He began with startling statistics, which he quoted without notes. His percentages and facts didn't seem stale or dry because he related each one to our current situation in America. He spoke with power and wisdom and humor.

His message was a call to America to come back to the principles of our founding fathers. As he was ending, he said, "I want us to pray for America."

My first thought was that he had found a good ending. It was appropriate. Prayer is the key to change and transformation. Having the audience pray for the country was a fitting and well-crafted ending.

But then the speaker surprised me. He said, "Before we pray, I want to tell you a story."

"As a young man, I started in ministry as the musician for a famous evangelist. We traveled around the world with a team and held big stadium evangelistic events. I was a successful musician, and I seemed to have a knack for leading praise and worship, but for months, I struggled because I felt God's call to become a preacher. The team was completing an event in Ireland and leaving for Russia the next day. That night, I told the evangelist about my feelings to become a preacher instead of a singer. The evangelist said, 'If you are going to leave me, do it now!'

"The team left for Russia, and I stayed in Ireland. I was young, inexperienced, and had no plan and no money.

"One morning the phone rang. It was the pastor of a church in Belfast. He said, 'Laddie, I hear you are going to preach now. Will you come to our church and preach a revival starting next week?'

"I said, 'Yes.'

"But the pastor continued. 'I don't think many people will come. Our people don't like revivals.'

"'Do you have anyone who will meet me at the church on Sunday evening to pray?' I asked.

'Yes, I can get a few.'

"A group of people met to pray for revival, and we prayed all night and into Monday morning. When Monday night came, the crowds were so big it was standing room only. Lives were changed, and the revival lasted for weeks."

After telling this story, the preacher looked at the audience and said, "A lot has happened to me in my life, and I may not be sure of a lot of things, but because of that experience in Ireland, I am sure about the power of prayer. Now, will you come and pray with me for America?"

Yes, we did. Hundreds of us left our seats and knelt at the altar to pray for our country.

The impact of his closing was phenomenal. The first closing that I thought he was making was appropriate and made the point. The story closing was stunning and memorable and made us understand the power of prayer. What a difference!

CLOSINGS MATTER

Your closing statement or story will be the challenge or encouragement your audience needs. Choose a technique and consider your objective. What challenge or hope do you want to leave with your group? Craft the ending well.

CHAPTER 9
RIGHT IN THE FUNNY BONE

"IF YOU WANT TO TELL PEOPLE THE TRUTH, MAKE THEM LAUGH, OTHERWISE THEY'LL KILL YOU." ~ OSCAR WILDE

Neither this book, nor any coach, can make you funny, but you can add wit and winsomeness to your presentations. And getting people to laugh is easier than you may think it is. Speaker coach, Craig Valentine says, "Don't add humor, uncover it."

If you want to teach truth in a fresh way, find humor because when they laugh, the audience gives themselves permission to open their minds. You will bond with the audience in a way no other technique can accomplish.

BUT I'M NOT FUNNY

If you can laugh, then you can be funny. Finding humor for your presentation is a matter of perspective. What seems humorous to you? Watch for opportunities to add wit and sparkle to your presentation.

You will be surprised how much humor and absurdity is in your daily life. Sometimes the most heart-wrenching places can have the most humorous elements. My friend's late father-in-law had to be moved to the dementia unit of a local nursing home. Visiting drained my friend and her husband emotionally, and they often shed tears, but the unit was also the source of many humorous memories. One time a female patient, in a burst of joyful exuberance, disrobed at the lunch table. Another patient insisted on having my friend carry imaginary packages across the room, and another day the same patient asked her to marry him. Laughter and tears are closely related.

Everyone does something ridiculous now and then. Pay attention. A friend finished sweeping her walk, so she carried the broom with her to the mailbox. On her way back from the mailbox, she suddenly spied some leaves under a bush and used her broom to dislodge them. One task led to another and the next thing you know, she was sweeping her yard with the broom.

Practice looking at the world the way children do. Be curious and open. Live "in the mood" to have fun. Keep your notebook handy to record those humorous moments. Then connect the humor to your topic.

Never tell jokes; you don't need them. Your life is funnier than any joke. In my notebook, I've recorded funny signs; hilarious words and actions from the children in my life; and the silly antics I've observed at sporting events, the local mall, and church. Keep your eyes and ears open and your pen ready. You'll have more material than you can use.

Here is a sign we saw on a country road. I howled with laughter when I saw it and we backed up so we could get a photo.

Once I saw this sign on a pole. I don't know what a "yale" is but it appears to be some kind of hybrid between a garage sale and a yard sale.

Actual signs like these are priceless. A joke is never as funny as reality.

Surprise Your Audience

Ken Davis says humor has three elements: surprise, exaggeration, and discovered truth. When you want to tell a funny story, you want to surprise your audience. You don't want them to know what is coming. Surprise your audience by putting down a verbal rug, convincing them it is safe, then yanking the rug out with the punch line. Exaggerate the elements of the story.

In a story about my grandmother's feather bed, I describe how you sink into the softness so deep that no one can see you. Exaggerated? Yes, but the audience feels the luxury of that thick mattress as I describe it. Then I tell them about the too-short slats that hold the mattress up and how you can't rest—because if you snuggle too deep and let your weight fully sink into the bed, you'll dislodge the slats and bed will fall. After you've exaggerated, you then find a way for the audience to discover the truth within the story. In the mattress story, I show how in God's rest we can truly rely on Him. When you do humor well, you will incorporate all three elements—surprise, exaggeration, and truth.

AUDIENCE CULTURE CAUTION

What is humorous in one country, state, county, or culture may not be funny in another. What is the culture where you are speaking? What gender is the crowd? Is there any language barrier that would keep them from understanding your humor? Make sure you are conscious of the age, values, styles, and interests of the audience. Then take the risk and add humor to your presentation. The Bible says, "A cheerful heart is good medicine" (Proverbs 17:22). Don't be boring and lifeless; insert your personality and include wit and winsomeness and humor.

LEARN ABOUT HUMOR

Comedians and professional humorists have studied the craft of humor carefully and have learned the techniques and timing. Learning the craft takes years of study and practice. Even the greatest of comedians show up at small improve theatres to practice their new material. Watch the people (professional or acquaintances) who you think are funny. Observe what styles and techniques work for them. Adapt what you see to your personality and style.

* * * * * * * * * * * * * * * *

COMEDY TECHNIQUES

Rule of Three

My friend, comedian Anita Renfroe, uses the rule of thirds when she says, "When Mama isn't home, dads feed the children things that end in o—Cheerios, Raviolios, and dominoes!" The crowd always laughs because they didn't expect the incongruent last item in the list of three. It's even funnier because the last word could mean small hard plastic toys or pizza. I've seen young moms call or text home to be sure all is well after that statement.

Picking the Right Word

Humorists know that hard consonants are funnier than soft consonants, so change words to add these hard sounds. Carrot instead of apple. Cottage instead of home.

Six Quick Tips

1) Learn the value of a pause for humorous effect. Often it is what you don't say or the quiet moment before the punch line that makes the humor successful. Using pauses is a powerful tool of timing.

2) Learn from comedians and other speakers who are funny, but don't copy them or try to retell their jokes. Learn the techniques that work such as looks, pauses, and body language. Watch the video of me telling about the name my grandchildren gave me. (Here is the link to the video: **https://www.youtube.com/watch?v=4E9rJNz-TENs&t=6s**) Notice the pause and facial expressions before I confirm the actual name.

3) Work within your style, personality, and demeanor. Use words, body language, facial expressions, and techniques that fit your skills and strengths. Notice when people laugh. Often in a presentation, something you say will tickle your audience even though you didn't expect it to be humorous. After you speak, analyze that moment. Why did they laugh? Perhaps it was the repetition of the statement or how the statement related to something you said earlier. Perhaps it was the inflection in your

voice or that the audience related it to another part of the program or some body movement you made. Figure out what worked, and plan to do it again.

4) Some humor in your presentation will be planned. You know it's funny, and it works with audiences and you have practiced it well. But some humor is organic and improvised. I teach a class on healthy eating. One night I proudly mentioned that my husband and I had resisted the temptation to stop at a favorite barbecue restaurant and went home to eat a taco salad. Later, when we calculated the calories, we discovered that our taco salad had a whopping 900 calories. The class laughed with me over our mishap, and I expected that. What I didn't expect was the number of times I could work in the words taco salad into the rest of my talk and get an instant laugh from the group.

5) Try to work in something humorous or light-hearted every five to seven minutes of your presentation.

6) The dangers of humor come when we give the secret (the punch line) away before the perfect moment in the story or when we set the story up wrong. Never say, "Oh, you're going to love this one," or, "I'm going to tell you a funny story." These sentences throw up a red flag to your audience who close their minds and think, You can't make me laugh.

If a story or funny line appears to be inappropriate, leave it out.

Give your audience permission to laugh, especially after a punch line. One of my favorite stories is about having my glamour shot made. After the elaborate set-up of how wonderful I looked in these photographs, I deliver the punch line, "My husband said, 'These are beautiful. Who is it?'" The audience howls if I give them permission. From my facial expression, they know I had laughed too.

Pause after the humorous line to allow your audience to laugh. But don't laugh at your own humor. If you get tickled, smile, then drop the microphone by your side so they won't hear you chuckle. If the humor fails, say something that rescues you. "Some of you will get that one on the way home." "Sorry, I'm from Texas." Famous comedians have planned lines or stances that save the day for them when the audience doesn't laugh. Johnny Carson's line was, "Some of these I just do for me." Milton Berle folded his arms and sighed an exasperated, "Well." Lucille Ball crossed her eyes and made a face.

SET THE MOOD FOR HUMOR

Use your opening as an opportunity to let your audience know you are there to spread joy. Set the tone for humor by creating a fun and funny atmosphere when you begin your presentation. Come on to the stage smiling.

IF YOU LOVE SPEAKING, NOTIFY YOUR
FACE. ~KAREN PORTER

Your body language and facial expressions will tell the audience they are going to enjoy their time with you. One speaker friend always wears outrageous colors or outfits for her humorous presentations.

You can even warm up your audience before you set foot on stage. At some events, especially if I am to speak several times, I will start a slide show before I come on stage. One of the slide shows is a collection of outrageous high-heeled shoes – everything from shoes that look like animals to high-heeled scuba flippers. When I come on stage after that slide show, the audience is ready to have fun. I also have a slide show called, "Why Husbands Shouldn't Babysit." It is a collection of fun photos of children covered in suds or drawings from markers or who are eating from the dog's bowl. The slide show is so funny, and every woman in attendance totally gets it. Some even call home to make sure all is well.

When you set the tone for fun, the audience will anticipate your humor. Use video bloopers, funny stories, self-depreciation, clips, or even quotes from Will Rogers or Yogi Berra. Make a collection that you can use to set the atmosphere before you speak.

Know the Punch Line

The key to good humor is practice, practice, practice. Try it out. Tune it up and then try again. Read funny articles; watch funny people; learn the techniques of humor, especially the technique of the pause, and apply these techniques to your personality and style.

"Humor is a rubber sword – it allows you to make a point without drawing blood." – Mary Hirsch

Chapter 10
On Techno Wings

"If God is in the details, then the Devil is in
PowerPoint." — @angrypaulrand

In this book, we won't go into all the technology you could use in a presentation. I encourage you to use media and technology that you can because both enhance presentations. Use video, audio, music, props, and visual aids if they help make your point and give the audience a great experience. Your audience is accustomed to slick media productions through TV, movies, the Internet, and in church. If you present with a lecture only, then you have missed an opportunity to connect visually and give auditory and visual stimulation to your audience.

Learn to use today's technology. Be familiar enough so you can troubleshoot problems with the microphone or computer or lighting. Learn to use whatever technology well enough that you can spot problems and fix them. But be prepared enough so that if your planned technology doesn't work, then you can give your presentation without the media dazzle. Don't rely on the media. If it goes wrong, do your presentation anyway.

LET'S TALK POWER POINT (OR KEY NOTE)

The Power Point is not your presentation; it augments and illustrates and makes your presentation more exciting. Do not rely on it so much that you can't give your speech if it fails. The audience came to hear you speak. Your PowerPoint is meant to enhance what you say. Unfortunately, this great tool (power point/keynote) has been misused in boardrooms and meeting rooms. Too many corporate meetings use tiny print, lots of words, and tiny intricate spreadsheets on a screen. No one can see or read the words, so the speaker reads the information. I can't imagine how boring this must be.

Author Nancy Duarte tell us, "My best advice is to not start [your preparation] in PowerPoint. Presentation tools force you to think through information linearly, and you really need to start by thinking of the whole instead of the individual lines." Bring the tool of PowerPoint into your preparation after you have developed your outline and your points and all the instructions, examples, and references. The slides will "add to" your presentation. Each slide should enhance the emotion, the effect, the facts of the presentation. If one of your outline points is to let the spirit flow in your spiritual life, use a photograph or video of a stream flowing or a waterfall or an open facet. Do not put a slide with only the words, "Let the Spirit Flow." Instead, allow the audience to feel the thought by seeing the flow of the water. If your outline point is about reaching the peak of your skill set, your slide should be the top of a mountain. The visual reinforcement of your words will help the audience understand and remember the point.

Author Garr Reynolds said, "Humans are completely incapable of reading and comprehending text on a screen and listening to a speaker at the same time. Therefore, lots of text (almost any text!) and long complete sentences are bad, Bad, BAD." Reynolds books, Presentation Zen and Presentation Zen Design are must reads for all speakers who use PowerPoint. Misusing this presentation tool can kill your presentation. Photographs, graphic visuals, video clips all work to give your audience the best experience without using words on the screen. Your audience cannot listen to what you say, look at their handouts, take notes, and read a screen full of written words all at the same time. If you must use words, use no more than two on a screen.

For example, in one presentation I stress that God never gives us a broad look at the future He has planned for us, but He expects us to take one step at a time. I show a full-screen photo of a forest. The underbrush, vines, and plants are so thick you could not move forward if you were there. This scene depicts how our next step looks to us—we cannot see the future. He only asks that we exert enough faith to take one step into the dense darkness. As we do, He opens up a path. In fact, if we take the steps one at a time in faith, he will make our path smooth. (See Psalm 119:105.) I always tell my audience that after we have taken those steps into the unknown future, we can turn around and see how God has opened the way. Then I show a photo of a lighted highway. The contrast between the two photos is a dramatic way for each person to see what God does when we step out in faith. The two photos emphasize your speech and handout—no words on the screen needed.

KEYS TO A GREAT POWERPOINT

- ☐ Pictures not words
- ☐ Few or no bullet points
- ☐ Big visual images or video clips
- ☐ Enhance not present

THE RULE OF THIRDS

Photographers understand and use the Rule of Thirds to produce great photos. The composition of the photo adheres to the rule by dividing up images into thirds, both vertically and horizontally. Think of the lines in a tick-tack-tow board. All main images or focal points in a photo or image must appear along the lines. Notice the four intersections of the lines. These spots are called Power Points. (I'm not kidding.) If you place your photos on these focal spots, you will have created a powerful and pleasing slide.

POWER POINTS

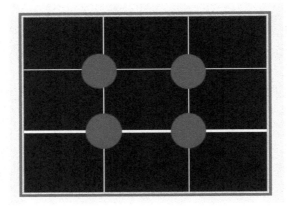

Videos

A well-placed video clip adds energy and more clarity to your presentation. Work with your equipment. Learn the software. Conquer the tool. Then check with your host to be sure the facility is equipped for media.

To use videos in PowerPoint, learn to embed the video. You can learn this skill by watching tutorial videos and reading the help pages. It is important to embed videos into your presentation rather than relying on the Wi-Fi or Internet connections which will cause delays because of buffering. The technology to embed videos isn't difficult. Learn it.

One of the most engaging church messages I ever heard was a sermon that compared a movie about a solo rock climber who got his hand wedged between two boulders to our life's choices. The presenter described portions of the story and then showed a short movie clip that captured just the point he wanted to make. He repeated the pattern about three times during his twenty- to thirty-minute presentation. Each clip was precisely chosen and edited. Before each clip, he prepared the audience by setting the scene without getting bogged down in details that didn't relate. After each clip, he made the analogy to our spiritual journey and choices. The vivid, well-used video made it a powerful presentation. And if the power had gone out in the room or if there had been some other technical glitch, I'm certain the speaker would have just kept going and told the story using descriptive language.

Never forget that the video clip is to supplement your presentation – not to be your presentation.

An awesome audio clip will capture an audience in a way nothing else can when used well. Consider a well-placed sound effect or dramatic music from a movie or symphony or a line or two from a song to enhance your point. Using audio of someone speaking is tricky unless it is short. Be careful not to use too-long segment, especially if all you have is voice.

Some speakers use a combination of audio and video and still photography to create a clever and meaningful presentation. Singer and actress Bonnie Keen uses a combination of video and live audio well in a presentation where her alter-ego (an on-screen Bonnie) argues with the in-person Bonnie on the stage. The effect is funny yet powerful.

What creative way could you use media in your next presentation?

You Job is to Become Tech Savvy

Take a class or go through tutorials on the Internet to learn as much as you can about the visual media you will use. Learn how to use audio and video and PowerPoint. The more you know, the less likely you will be to encounter problems. Learn your hardware, too. Buy the plugs, connections, and adapters that you will need. Practice putting it together to project the PowerPoint. Review and study the software. Google it to discover all the hacks and keyboard shortcuts. Find the best way to transport your PowerPoint to the event either 1) sending it via email or Dropbox prior to the event 2) using your personal computer or tablet as the source for the PowerPoint 3) transferring the PowerPoint to a portable device such as a thumb drive.

The more you understand, the better you can use the technology.

CHAPTER 11
OWNING YOUR STAGE

"IT'S STAGE PRESENCE THAT DISTINGUISHES A PRESENTER WHO CAN RELAY INFORMATION TO ONE WHO CAN SINGLE-HANDEDLY BRING THE AUDIENCE TO HIS SIDE." ~ DENNISON

You need to be aware and comfortable with the stage setting for your presentation. Arrive early at the venue where you will speak so you can check out the stage, the microphones, the podium, the lighting, and the general space.

My first rule is: Do not be a prima dona. Do not demand or make ultimatums that will cause your hosts to wish they'd never invited you. Instead, make the best of whatever situation by thinking carefully before you spout off the first need that comes into your mind. Seek to make the best scenario for that event. Ask nicely for changes in the stage arrangement or the lighting or the microphone, but never be demanding.

LIGHTING AND PODIUM

Before the event, as you stand on the stage, look at the lights. The best lighting is at 45-degree angles. If the lighting leaves you in a dark spot, talk to the technician and see if you can get it changed. If not, move to a different place on the stage to get better lighting that doesn't cause shadows.

If possible, remove the podium from the stage. If others are going to use the podium or you feel you must have some notes, try to get a short table placed on the stage for you. If the podium is the only thing available, ask someone to move it to the side so there is no barrier between you and the audience.

NEVER LEAN ON A PODIUM.

Your clothing, hairstyle, and appearance need to be neat and stylish. Women, be sure your makeup is appropriate for the situation. You may need more makeup than usual if the lights are strong. Men, make sure your tie is straight and check those zippers one more time.

Ask your assistant or a trusted friend to give you one last "look-over" before you go on stage. If everything is buttoned, zipped, and in place, walk on stage with confidence.

"WHEN IT'S A LIVE PERFORMANCE, ANYTHING CAN HAPPEN." ~ RENE ANGELIL

DANGER ON THE FLOOR

Pay attention to musical instruments, podiums, decorations, wires, speakers, and such are on the stage with you. Get familiar with it so you can move freely when you speak. Some stages will have holes under the carpet (perhaps for electrical cords) or the stage consists of sections, leaving gaps when they are put together.

Do a survey of the floor situation before the event and note any area that could catch your heel or toe and trip you while on stage. You can avoid these danger spots if you are aware of them.

Be gracious and kind to the tech staff and team members of the host group. Ask politely if something needs to be changed. Accept their solutions with grace and humility. No stage is perfect, and no event will be perfect either.

FINISH ON TIME

You must finish your presentation on time. Use a phone, watch, or countdown clock. Even if you start late because of someone else going too long, make the effort to finish according to the time on the program or schedule. It is the professional way to do it, and the event planner will love you for it. If you prepare your presentation using the techniques in this book such as P.I.E.R., you can give your message in ten minutes or thirty minutes because you only expand or shrink the message by the number of examples, instructions, and references you share.

CHAPTER 12
AT THE TOP OF YOUR VOICE

CHANGE YOUR VOICE—CHANGE YOUR LIFE
~ROGER LOVE

Your voice may hold you back from promotions in your job and from being successful as a speaker. The sound of our voices makes the right or wrong impression and affects how people perceive us.

Imagine enduring a boring monotone voice for a 30-40 minute presentation. As an audience member, you become lethargic and flat because of the sounds you hear. And even if the information is interesting, you do not uncover any enthusiasm for it. Imagine the same presentation with a speaker who mixes up the pitch of his voice and uses different volumes and pacing throughout the speech. And even if the information isn't as interesting, you will find some bit of it interesting and exciting.

A boring voice will not convince the audience.

Some researchers believe that the sounds the audience hears are more important than the impact of body language. And some studies show that the sound of your voice will convince the audience of the power of the information you are presenting—either for good or for bad. A nasally or high-pitched squeaky voice will negate any serious points you may make. A thick accent or drawl might cause the audience to pre-judge your intelligence. A deep voice in women sounds aggressive, but sounds like a leader in men. A breathy voice is hard to believe. A sharp, clear tone is pleasant.

Think of your voice like a band instrument. Each player in the band must tune to the pitch of the other instruments. If your voice is your message (a sad dreary voice talking about finding happiness) and out-of-tune with the hearers (the tone or quality annoys the audience). The volume of the voice sets the tone for the presentation (Screaming or whispering is not only bad for the vocal cords but also harmful to the audience's ears). I watched a video about how to care for herbs in my garden. At the end of each sentence, the speaker added an upward lilt to the last word. The result was a sing-song quality that bothered me so much I quit watching the video. I heard a woman speak with "barbie doll" inflections and wide-eyed faux innocence. I didn't take her seriously. I heard a different woman speak in harsh tones, which made me feel she was angry.

Speak in a clear, strong voice so that the audience doesn't miss one word. Getting the most out of your voice may require some work and some practice, but the results are worth it. You will keep your audience's attention, your habits won't annoy them, and your talk will have an energy that captivates. The keys are volume, pitch, and pace. Listen to yourself in a recorded presentation. Are your words and sentences too fast? Are you too slow? Work on getting a varied pace and never speak so fast the audience can't understand your words.

Project Your Words

Most speakers voices aren't loud enough, even with a microphone. Speak louder. Some speakers absorb the sounds of their voice into the throat. It sounds as if they are gulping the words. This keeps the tone muted and gives the effect of swallowing the words. Practice pushing the words out of the front of your mouth to project each word. Practice pronouncing the ending consonants in words. Ask a friend to help you as you try this experiment. Go into an auditorium-sized room and stand on the stage with no microphone. Ask your friend to go to the back of the room. Speak so that your friend can understand and hear every word. Practice speaking in that tone.

VARY YOUR VOLUME

Our voices have three volume levels: normal, minimum, and maximum. A normal tone is the loudness of your voice when you speak in a conversational tone. Softer than that normal tone is your minimum voice—the softest you can speak and still be heard. Louder than that normal tone is your maximum voice, the loudest you can speak without shouting. You should use all three tones in your presentations. Practice out loud to determine what each of the three levels feels like. Then use them appropriately throughout your presentation. Levels of volume bring texture to your presentations. All three volume levels must have strong energy support, which means you must breathe deeply and pronounce the words and project the tone even in the softest voice.

LEARN TO BREATHE

Support your voice and your words with plenty of air. Inhaling without raising your shoulders will fill your diaphragm. Put your hands on each side of your waist, and see if you can feel your diaphragm (just below your rib cage) expanding. Watch yourself in a mirror to be sure you don't raise your shoulders. If you have trouble understanding how to support your voice with your breath, talk to a trained musician. The person who sings in your church has studied how to use good breathing techniques and can help you add power to your voice. If you want to experience how correct breathing feels, lie down on your back on a piano bench or similar hard surface. Then breathe deeply—you will naturally use your diaphragm in this position. When you fill your diaphragm, your voice will take on a deeper, richer quality.

"EVERY SINGLE PERSON NEEDS TO BREATHE IN THROUGH THEIR NOSE, FILL UP THEIR TUMMY AS IF THE AIR WAS GOING IN THERE, AND THEN SPEAK WHILE THEIR STOMACH IS COMING IN. ~ ROGER LOVE

You need power behind your words. Fill your softest voice with energy and strength.

WARM UP

Before a presentation, warm up – much like singers do prior to a concert. Memorize a few tongue twister lines and repeat them out loud to warm up your voice.

Here are some lines which actors practice when warming up before a play: These tongue twisters are meant to help you pronounce consonants and vowels. Practice these fast and slow. Practice them until you have memorized the words. When you warm up your voice with exercises like this, your voice and your enunciation will improve dramatically.

Whaa Ta
To   Do
To   Die
To   Day
At   A
Minute
Or   Two
Til   Two

* * *

A   Thing
Distinctly
Hard
To   Say
But   Harder
Still
To   Do

* * *

But To Beat
A Taboo
At Twenty Til Two
At A Rat-TATA-TATA-TATA-TATA-TATA-TATA-TATA
Too

* * *

And The Dragon
Will Come At The
Beat Of A Drum
At A Minute Or Two
Til Two Today

Forget Filler Words

As you speak, watch for filler words. *And. Ah. Uh. So.* All these words are sounds that come out of your mouth when you are thinking about what to say next. It is much better not to make any sound at all than to fill the space with these pesky words.

Some speakers develop a word habit. They use some term repeatedly, often without hearing the word themselves. The term shows up when the speaker is nervous or trying to fill dead space in the air. Some of those word habits are words like Amen? Or Okay? These words show up at the end of every sentence and serve only to annoy the audience.

Once I was coaching a client, and my friend and mentor Florence Littauer listened in. Afterwards, she pulled me aside and said, "You said the words *'you know'* nine times in one minute." I was unaware that I ever used that filler phrase. In fact, that one phrase annoys me more than any other. I was unhappy that I had picked up this habit. She gave me a great tip on how to stop using such terms. She said, "Give your brain an assignment: Brain, every time you hear me say those two words, call it to my attention."

I followed her advice and gave my brain that assignment. Now, if I hear those two words come out of my mouth, my brain hears it, and I adjust so that the two words won't slip out again.

If you have a habit word, you can stop saying it. Begin by giving your brain an assignment. It is amazing what your brain can do in the background while you are giving a speech.

Use Energy and Rich Tone

Your voice must have energy and richness, or your audience will not stay with you for a full presentation. A high-pitched voice grates on the audience's ears. A gravelly voice becomes unpleasant quickly.

Use the breathing techniques mentioned earlier to help give your voice a more rounded quality. Speak from the diaphragm. Let the vowels form in your mouth and project the words out with crisp beginning and ending consonants. Use pauses and timing well. Some points need a brief pause to be fully appreciated. Punch lines and quotations often need a pause at the end to allow the line or thought to soak into the minds of your audience. Practice pausing. Be sure the timing of all phrases is clear. Some statements need to be stated fast. Other phrases need to be slowed down.

Practice Speaking Scripture

I believe reading or quoting Scripture is one of the most important moments on stage. Never read a passage unless you have read it out loud many times before. Practice the words and the phrases. Be able to pronounce every word clearly without hesitation. Practice reading out loud so that you will read God's Word well.

Perform Your Best

In Christian circles it isn't considered good form to call your presentation, speech, sermon, lesson, or talk a performance, but don't be fooled into thinking it is okay to be mediocre. Your audience is well-acquainted with professional performance in every area of life from TV programs and movies to events at work and on the Internet. If your words are put together poorly and you don't have a strong point and an interesting way to present it, then they have no real reason to listen. If you practice and you study the craft of speaking, then you will give your presentation with the skill of a professional performer, and you will have the Holy Spirit to bless and anoint you, and the audience will receive the message.

When Jesus went into the synagogue in Capernaum, He read the Scriptures like the people had never heard them read before;

He spoke truth to the people with authority and power, and He left them breathless. You can do the same if you work hard on your voice and the energy and skills you need.

CHAPTER 13
SOMETHING IN THE WAY YOU MOVE

"THE ARTS MAKE A BRIDGE ACROSS THIS WORLD IN WAYS THAT
NOTHING ELSE CAN." ~ JULIE ANDREWS

In theatre, the director plans and paces each movement. The methods an actor uses to develop the character he or she is portraying in the scene show in the movement. The character may move quickly or slowly, heavily, lightly, haltingly, or deliberately. The movements tell the audience something about the character's emotion, ambition, and feelings. The director works out a plan—called blocking—so that each actor is in the exact spot on stage for the next line. The actor can project inner thoughts, emotions, needs, and wants by using his or her body in motion. The actor considers how the character will walk, such as leading from different points in the body—the chin, stomach, pelvis and how much the character will swing his or her arms or lift his feet—and how the character will stand still.

Move with Purpose

Use the stage as part of your message. Every inch of the platform is an empty canvas waiting for you to paint the picture for your audience. Movement is a sign of life. Moving on a stage is a good method but pacing back and forth or rocking from heel to toe is distracting. Move with purpose. Walk to one side of the stage and look at the crowd. Finish the thought or sentence before you turn to move again. After you have finished the thought, walk to the middle or the other side of the stage. Always look in the direction you are going. Never walk one direction and look the other direction. Your position on stage becomes part of your presentation.

Neutral

While movement is good, it is also important to find a neutral place on the stage—a place you can park. This spot should be where you start your presentation and the place you return when you move. This spot is neutral. Go there often.

In addition, find a comfortable body position that will become your neutral position. Take that stance often, too. It may be hands at your side or in some other comfortable natural position. When you make a hand gesture to emphasize a point, return to neutral as soon as possible.

Be cautious of your movements in a room that is fan shaped. If the stage is circular and there are people on both sides to the extreme left and right, you may have a tendency to pace back and forth because of the wide area of the crowd. Force yourself to stand still and then move to each side with purpose.

I'm asking you to move with purpose, but I understand this stage principle presence is hard. I have practiced it over and over to get the perfect balance between movement and standing still. Yet I recently spoke in a church auditorium, which had an audience seating arrangement of about 180 degrees. Even though I knew better, the video of that event shows me walking back and forth as I try to include every audience member every time. The result was frenetic pacing. Make a conscious effort to limit your pacing and movements. This skill will take time and practice.

Concentrate on standing still. Nervous pacing even one step each way or rocking back-and-forth worries and distracts your audience.

In our presentations, we are not playing the part of a written character; we are revealing ourself as the leader, speaker, trainer, preacher, teacher, expert. What we do with our body exposes whether we are authentic. We can plan movements and gestures but if we don't do them well, we will be perceived as fake, awkward, artificial.

The speaker battles between planned movement and habitual actions. Movement must feel fluid to be perceived as natural and organic—not planned. But if movement isn't planned, habit takes over—which is often erratic and sloppy. You've seen the person on stage who paces back and forth with no reason for the movement? That's habit, not natural. You've seen the speaker whose hands flail around in every direction? It's probably a nervous habit. You've also seen the speaker whose practiced movements seem robotic. Speakers need a balance between the two extremes.

You might think it would be better to stand in one spot since movement can be treacherous, but standing glued to one spot on the stage ignores all the wonderful points on the stage that can reach your audience on new levels. Movement helps you reach every person in the audience. If you move to the side where they are sitting or come down from the stage to the aisles where their seats are, you will connect with each person there.

Center stage is your strongest area on the stage, but you don't want to live there.

You are on the stage to connect with the people in the audience. You need the connection—the interaction—with them so you can communicate the facts and inspiration of your presentation.

POSTURE

Begin with a basic stance:

1) Feet as wide as your hips (feet together generally signify insecurity—wider stance equals confidence).

2) Stand as tall as possible. Straight but relaxed. Relax your shoulders.

3) Pull your shoulders back.

4) Keep a tension within your core, but move with grace.

This basic stance should feel like a comfortable position. Pacing or rocking annoys your audience who will focus on your movements, not on what you say. In contrast, standing too straight and too still will lull your audience into a trance. Find a midway point between slouching and standing stiffly and formally. If you relax your stance and seem composed and unruffled, you will invite the audience into your world. They will relax, knowing they are in your good hands, and they can trust you.

It is rarely a good move to put your hands in your pockets or cross your arms. Sometimes men can put their hands into a pocket for a casual look, but don't give your entire presentation with your hands in your pocket. Be sure there is no loose change or keys in your pocket to rattle. Face the audience as much as possible.

"PEOPLE WON'T REMEMBER WHAT YOU SAY AS MUCH AS THEY WILL REMEMBER WHAT THEY SEE WHEN YOU TALK." ~PATRICIA FRIPP

What you say and how you say it is only part of your presentation. A big percentage of what you communicate in your presentation is nonverbal. If you are nervous and pacing or slumped over with bad posture, then you will convey a message that may differ from your words. Your body will give out a stronger message than your voice.

Feel the Audience

A key to great communication is to make the audience feel comfortable with you. One way you can help your audience relax and become comfortable with you is to remove any barriers that separate you from them. Remove the podium or stand. If it is unmovable, spend most of your time in front of it or beside it. Standing behind a podium, especially if it is large, will separate you from those who came to hear you speak. A podium separates you from the audience and reading your material will bore them. Be so prepared that you need no notes, or at the least no more than one small card with a few prompts.

Use Meaningful Hand Movements

Find a comfortable, neutral position for your hands. Try to hold them at your sides in a casual way. Do not put them together at your waist and play spider olympics with your fingers. Instead, place your hands at your sides and then use one or both of them to make a point. You are not required to illustrate everything you say with your hands. Instead, make movements for the most important points.

Every movement of your hand should be purposeful. Hand motions will illustrate and support, or they will distract and annoy. Purposeful hand movements make your point. Habitual or repetitive hand movements may stop your audience from hearing your point. Don't move half-heartedly, as if you are too timid to express yourself. Sweep your hands when saying "everything" or reach up high when saying, "God in heaven," or fold your arms across your chest when saying, "I refused." When you add these hand gestures, they are powerful, especially if you start and stop the movement with a return of your hands to your neutral position. Purposeful hand movements are much more powerful than fidgety hands going in many directions with no purpose.

Never pump your hands, repeating a movement without purpose. Too many speakers use their hands to emphasize every word in a staccato beat to go with the rhythm of their words. I've noticed this tendency, especially if the speaker is using a hand-held microphone. Such speakers seem compelled to pump the other hand to emphasize their words. These movements mean nothing and become a distraction. It is far better to put your hand to your side and then use the hand to make deliberate, meaningful movements that truly illustrate the words you are saying.

Nerves can get the best of anyone, so practice your neutral position. Be conscious that your hands don't contradict your words. Always hold up the proper number of fingers for whatever number you want to illustrate. Your audience will lose confidence in you if you say "three" while holding up only two fingers.

I often tell a favorite story about the lights going off and on during a storm. I hold my hands up high, then I open and close them to illustrate the off-on of the lights. One day, my husband said, "Karen, you need to work on that hand motion. You are closing your fingers when you say the lights went on and opening your fingers when the lights went off." I practiced and practiced until I got the hand motion right. Now, in the instant before I start that movement, I make sure I start with the lights off first so my hands will be consistent with my story. Be sure your hand movements match your words.

ILLUSTRATE WITH YOUR WHOLE BODY

Your body illustrates the message. If you are telling a story with two characters, you can differentiate them by your body language. If one is powerful and confident, then stand tall and speak loudly. If the other is shy or afraid, then show it in your body stance and voice inflection. Using this technique is like being an actor in a one-person show; you need to become each character in your story. It can take practice to become adept at switching back and forth between characters, but don't give up. Your stories will come alive if you use body language to your advantage.

NEVER READ YOUR MANUSCRIPT

Reading your presentation is a sure way to kill it. Never—ever—read your message. If your audience wanted only to read your words, they would have bought your book and not bothered to come to your presentation.

Reading your manuscript bores all audiences.

I attended one event along with several thousand people. The speaker was well-known and successful. When he came on stage, he looked great. He carried a large black three-ring binder, which he placed on the podium. He began to read his message. The words were beautiful and meaningful, and he read with great dramatic flair, but he lost the audience because we never saw his face as his head was buried in the binder. During the reading, he came to a section about witnessing. He read, "We must tell others about the salvation God offers." He looked up at the audience and in a moment of exuberance, he came from behind the podium, jumped down from the stage and approached several people up the aisle saying, "You gotta tell somebody! You gotta tell somebody!" He was enthusiastic and full of life and joy as he got excited about evangelism.

Then, as if he suddenly realized what he'd done, he straightened up, went back on stage, and began reading again. What a shame. He had wonderful inspiration to say and a dramatic voice, but his stage presence behind the podium never allowed us in the audience to connect with him or his message.

MAKE EYE CONTACT

Your eyes are the windows to your soul. If the audience never sees your eyes, then they will never see the depths of who you are and will never believe your message. You connect to them with your eyes.

Look at the audience—not above their heads or at the back of the room. Look directly into the eyes of one audience member at a time. No sweeping the room allowed.

As I watch speakers, eye contact is the one thing that rarely happens. The speaker scans the room right to left but never looks directly at any one person.

If I stand on stage and sweep my eyes over the audience from right to left, it appears as if I am looking at the people. What I'm actually seeing is shapes and colors—a tall outline of green, blue, pink; a shorter outline of gold; a crowded section; yellow; the shape of a beard; yellow, brown; an empty section. I see the room, but not any specific individual. Sweeping the audience this way will prevent me from connecting with the audience and they with me.

Looking into the eyes of individuals, one person at a time, is the key to connecting with the audience. Connecting in this way will make your presentations conversational, and people will relate to you and your message.

Research shows that if a speaker looks directly into the eyes of a person in a crowded audience, the people around that person feel the connection too. Each one will feel as if you are talking directly to him or her.

Hold the eye contact until you finish the thought. Look at someone else directly in the eyes, make your point, and finish that thought before you look away. Even if they look away, keep looking at them. Your message will come through strong and clear in a way you never dreamed possible.

I worked with a client who led a small group of about twenty people. After I taught her about the power of eye contact, she tried it on her small group. She was amazed and thrilled at the result. The group opened up in discussion like never before. When the event was over, one person came up to her and said, "Wow, you learned a lot when you went to that workshop. You've never been this powerful before." My client swears the only technique she changed was eye contact, and it made all the difference in the event.

Use Your Body, Hands, and Eyes with Purpose

Body and hand language speak loudly. Use both purposefully. Using eye contact well will revolutionize your stage presence and your speaking success.

CHAPTER 14
SHOW YOU ARE A PRO

"HOW YOU FIRST MEET THE PUBLIC IS HOW THE INDUSTRY
SEES YOU. YOU CAN'T ARGUE WITH THEM. THAT'S THEIR
PERCEPTION." ~MERYL STREEP

Novelist J.K. Rowling said, "A good impression can work wonders." She's right because how people observe you when you arrive on stage is how they will perceive your presentation. You can't argue with them about what they should think, and it is difficult to change that first impression. Listed below are eight steps to looking like a pro.

Step 1—Preparation is key to a great presentation. Mark Twain said, "It usually takes me more than three weeks to prepare a good impromptu speech." Work hard on your outline, your stories, your instructions, and find the best references. Put the presentation together in a logical and interesting way. Know much more on the subject than you can present. Billy Graham said that he studied himself full and then wrote until he was empty and then studied until he was full again. Then and only then he preached. To give a power-packed thirty-minute presentation requires you to know hours' worth of material.

Step 2—Your message will carry as much authority and punch as you believe it will carry. Do you believe the message? Have you practiced the concepts? Have you implemented the ideas? Your audience will see you as an authority on a subject if you know much more than you present in your speech. Study all the topics that influence your topic, such as how other cultures are affected. How does your topic affect all ages or all personality types? If you have consumed information and background about your topic, your knowledge will fill your presentation with strong undertones that your audience can sense.

Believe your material. Don't speak on a subject unless you are sold on the facts and certainty of the material. If it is a theological truth, have you embraced in your life? If it is an action step, are you willing to make the first move? When you believe what you speak, power and authority fill your presentation.

Step 3—Use the best words. Use strong verbs and colorful descriptions to make your presentation interesting and powerful. Convince your hearers with the best images and metaphors. Persuade your audience with compelling language. You have five senses; use each one in your presentation. Become an observer of your world. Pay attention to the colors, textures, sounds, smells, and images around you. The success of your stories depends on how you transport your audience to the scene. Help them experience the setting.

If I told you about a trip to the beach, I could describe the day as hot and the beach as crowded and the waves coming in one after another. Then I could challenge the audience to take a break from busyness and go to a beach to sit and watch the waves. The audience might get the idea that we need to take time to rest and relax. But few would remember the story or be excited about the possibility. But if I want you to enter the story with all your senses, I might tell you about the beach trip like this:

We drove the convertible to the beach as if we were young and carefree. I held tight to the braided edge of my big-brimmed hat. When we arrived at the water's edge, we carried our picnic lunch and umbrella and chairs to the sand. Two men who had the same bald head and the same blond mustache set up tents for their families nearby—brothers on a mini family reunion. The children squealed with laughter as their toes touched the salty sea. The tantalizing smell of burgers on a grill filled the air as we savored our ham sandwiches and watermelon. I stared at the waves for hours, thinking of adjectives I could use to describe their never-ending movement. Rolling—yes, they rolled in. Breaking—beginning far out into the ocean where a sand bar had formed. Rushing—even knocking some people down as they stood in the surf. Never ending.

The scene is a snapshot of life. We are busy like the waves, never stopping or taking a breath or a break. Life comes at us hard, and as soon as we have faced one crashing wave, another hits us from behind. On the beach, I watched the waves for hours. Instead of being in the middle of the chaos, I rested, relaxed, observed, and enjoyed. We need days like that when we are an observer. When we step away from the rush of life.

Did you see the five senses in my revised story—seeing, hearing, smelling, touching, and tasting? Using the senses to describe the scene makes the story come alive, and your points will be strong and memorable.

Step 4—Condense for Clarity. After suggesting you use details and descriptions, I now caution about using too many details in your stories. It is easy to allow charming or funny details to take over the story and lose the point of the story. Every story must have a point, but your point will get lost in a 30-minute story. And since most presentations are no more than 30-40 minutes, a long story will sabotage your presentation. Edit every story. Prune every description. Remove unnecessary repetition. Keep the details, the repetition, the descriptions that liven up your story and get rid of anything that slows it down.

Step 5—Convince the audience of your point instead of entertaining them with your story. I was set to give a preliminary speech before a panel of coaches. The time limit for the speech was 5 minutes. I wanted to give one point for the brief presentation. The best example I had for the point was a story that typically takes three and one-half minutes to tell. (Yes, I had timed it.) But this story would dominate my five minutes, so I condensed and cut and trimmed the story. I took out details I loved but took too much time. I sliced and diced the dialogue in the story to the bare minimum. I shortened the story to two minutes. But it was still too long, so I sharpened my editor's pencil. I pruned the story down to 90 seconds and used it in my five-minute speech. The shortened version didn't lose the flavor of the story and still had good descriptions and funny lines. The story still made my point. I filled the rest of my five minutes with references and instructions. I received a great critique from the coaches.

Your challenge is to edit your story to include succinct, captivating descriptions that fascinate your audience and convince them of your point or the action you want them to take. Ask yourself: "How short can I make this story?" And like me, you may learn which details are the most important in your story.

Step 6—If you want to be a pro, then dress like a pro. I always suggest you dress like the crowd with a bit more care. Wear a jacket if the attendees are dressed casually. Wear jeans with a great sweater if the weather is cool and the location is a camp. Don't overdress or underdress.

Step 7—Be respectful of the audience. Craft your presentation to help the audience. Speak words that help them understand you are a fellow traveler. If you've struggled with the concepts, let them know instead of presenting yourself as someone who is perfect.

Step 8—Give them more than they expected. Uncover the humor in your presentation. Issue challenges to your audience. Help them see how authentic and realistic you are.

A professional speaker is competent and reliable. Every word spoken from the stage instills confidence and helps the audience believe what you will say next. If you are organized, confident, positive, honest, ethical, and knowledgeable, they will listen carefully.

Chapter 15
Swim with the Current

LIFE IS LIKE RIDING A BICYCLE. TO KEEP YOUR BALANCE, YOU MUST KEEP MOVING. ~ALBERT EINSTEIN

A few years ago, my book *I'll Bring the Chocolate* was published. Since then, I have traveled the country speaking to hundreds of women's groups in churches and other venues. The book compares all the luscious qualities of women's friendships to all the luscious qualities of chocolate.

Many of these events are elaborate girls-night-out-chocolate parties. The attendees come for a night of relaxation and fun, and a chocolate party gives the women an opportunity to get away from the stress of jobs and responsibility and for an hour or so to laugh and relax. I have developed several chocolate presentations full of humorous stories and give the audience just what they expect—a lot of fun. The events are a success. I enjoy myself at these events and, frankly, it is invigorating to hear the crowds laugh as I present my humor. Okay, I'll admit it, I've even felt a bit of pride that I can be so entertaining. It is easy for my sanguine personality type to get caught up in the excitement.

One morning, after weeks of successful events, I sat in my

favorite chair to read my Bible. As I meditated on the passage and prayed, I sensed God's reprimand. "Karen, I didn't call you to be a comedienne."

Yes, God made me a little funny, but He didn't intend my presentations to be shallow or fluffy. My calling is to present relevant truth that changes hearts and behaviors and points to Jesus. I can fulfill my purpose in a pleasant, even a funny way—but being funny isn't my primary role.

Although the book *I'll Bring the Chocolate* is full of fun stories and chocolate recipes, it also contains rich spiritual truths about faith, loyalty, forgiveness, and encouragement. When I speak in a retreat setting and have three or four sessions to delve into these concepts deeply, I like to help the women understand deep spiritual concepts. But I fell short of my calling in the one-talk, girls-night-out events.

I reworked my presentations to include the richer and deeper concepts along with the fun. Lesson learned: Never stop tweaking the content and delivery of your presentations. Stay current, relevant, and true to your calling. Don't speak fluff and tell pointless stories—no matter how entertaining they might be or how much you like the story—unless they make your point. People are hurting. People need answers. Speakers who adopt deep, spiritual certainty as the basis of each presentation are able to speak significant and beneficial truth.

CURRENT

As speakers, we need to be up to date.

Before you go on stage, be sure you have read today's newspaper or an online news source. Be aware of recent tragedies, world crisis events, big sports news, and even celebrity news. You may or may not use the news in your presentation, but being unaware of it could be disastrous. Also, check out the local news for the community or city where you are speaking. Being uninformed about a local tragedy such as a car accident involving local high school kids could be embarrassing or awkward, and you could miss a ministry opportunity.

The best way to know your audience is to ask the event planner or team questions about the community, the people, and the sponsor of the event. Here are some questions to ask:

1) How many people do you expect to attend?

2) What is the average age group?

3) Will the audience be men or women or both?

4) Describe the community (urban, rural, suburbs)

5) What are the major industries in the area?

6) Are the majority of the attendees business owners, employees, or retired?

7) What sports do the people follow? Local, college, professional?

8) How long has the organization—non-profit, business, or church—been in existence?

9) Ask the event planner to describe the group of people (active, long-time members, new group etc).

You will be more informed and can adapt your presentation to the needs of the group.

Up to Date

Immerse yourself in the latest technology so those attending the event will know you are modern and apt. We will go in-depth into on-stage technology in chapter 10 but use the checklist below to ensure that you are able to navigate the world of devices and the Internet if you want to be taken seriously as a speaker.

CHECKLIST

- ☐ You have a website – using your name as the domain name if possible
- ☐ You have an email address using your name
- ☐ You have developed a brand and a mission statement.
- ☐ You have a tag line which states your brand in a short pithy statement
- ☐ You know how to use transfer programs such as Dropbox, Adobe, Google docs so you can send your photo and biographical materials to event planners
- ☐ You have a presence on social media platforms – Facebook, Twitter, Instagram, Pinterest, LinkedIn and others
- ☐ You have professional photos, both headshots and action shots
- ☐ You know how to use meeting software such as Zoom, Skype, and Google meet.
- ☐ You have good lighting and backgrounds for videos and on-line meetings
- ☐ You know how to produce a quality video greeting the audience prior to an upcoming event
- ☐ You have promotional materials to send to the event planner
- ☐ You have a professional contract to send to the event planner

FRESH

At the beginning of this book, I mentioned a lady named Florence Littauer. She was an international speaker and author of dozens of books. She also trained more than 30,000 speakers in her career, including many famous communicators you would know and me. Toward the end of her public speaking career, the Advanced Writers and Speakers Association honored her with a lifetime achievement award. She spoke to the group, most of whom she had trained and encouraged. She gave her most requested and most famous presentation, which included parts of her amazing life story. Though I had heard this presentation numerous times and she had given thousands of times, she told her story with new, innovative life applications. Those of us who listened and knew the story felt as if we were hearing it for the first time, because she spoke with joy and enthusiasm—and a freshness that caused all of us to marvel.

Let's summarize the ways to keep our messages crisp and fresh and full of energy and passion.

1) Watch how culture is changing by observing people, entertainment, and news.

2) Keep short accounts with God through daily time with Him learning more about Him and His character and attributes.

3) Stay (or get) physically healthy. Exercise will make you strong and healthy. Eating healthy foods will build your stamina for the long hours of travel in uncomfortable airplanes and enhance your energy, endurance, and resilience—and make you appear vibrant on stage.

4) Build your presentation with fresh, passionate, lively words, eliminating clichés and tired religious words. Some "spiritual language" is so tired and old that we have become experts at saying almost nothing. Avoid overused words peculiar to the Christian faith. Consider fresh ways to say some of the most common Christian phrases.

5) Choose applicable topics as you prepare your presentation. How does your audience need this message? What are the best stories to make the point? What do people *think* they need, and what do they *really* need?

TRENDS

What is your audience thinking about today? What do they want to know now? There are numerous places to search online that will give you an overview of what is trendy today.

1) www.google.com/trends. On this site, you will explore what the world is searching for that day. The site shows you the top searches, and it updates several times a day. You will see real-time answers for the questions the world is asking. On a big sports day, the trend relate to sports. For example, Super Bowl day or NBA signing day. Watch these trends for fresh, current, viable fodder to which you can refer.

2) www.trendhunter.com. The site contains the top trends presented by category. You will see a daily dose of micro trends, viral news, and pop culture and what's hot for the next holiday and what collectors are searching for. If you want to know the top ten favorite ice cream flavors or the top 50 automobile trends in a month, this site will probably have it for you. The categories on this site include fashion, tech, life, culture, design, ads, business, luxury, and others.

3) www.twitter.com#trends. On twitter, the hashtag #trends will help you find the latest hot topic being discussed on twitter.

4) www/indeed.com/jobtrends. You can find the latest employment news and job information.

5)   www.style.com/trendsshopping. You will see the latest on fashion and upcoming seasons.

6)   www.coolest-gadgets.com. See all the newest stuff in the techie world and other industries.

7)   www.coolhunting.com. This site covers all the latest in design, technology, style, travel, art, and culture.

Keeping current is important for fresh and interesting presentations.

Chapter 16
Sweet Spots, Buzz Words, & Your Zone

"Out of the fullness of his grace he has blessed us all, giving us one blessing after another" (John 1:16 GNB).

There is a moment—a suspension in time when I stand on stage in front of an audience—that I feel it ... my sweet spot. This tick in time is when the abilities unique to me, the talents God gave me, my personality type, and my training put me in that sphere. I know at that moment I am doing what I'm supposed to be doing, and I am standing in the middle of God's will for my life.

Some might describe this sweet place as an anointing, which is defined as "influence, motivation, inspiration." Author and pastor Max Lucado said, "When God gives an assignment, He also gives the skills." A well-prepared, well-ordered, backed-by-the-truth speech presented by a person with talent and skills produces the sweet spot in communicators.

While all of us share some stage fright moments, if you shutter and shake and fear the stage, then that might be a sign that speaking isn't for you. Being prepared solves fear and anxiety. Once I get over those first step-on-the-stage butterflies, my fear goes away, and my connection with the audience begins.

Perhaps you can understand the idea of sweet spot if I use the word connection, which may be more descriptive of this feeling. Connection brings those ah-ha moments between the speaker and the audience. If I have prepared my presentation thoroughly, and I'm using all the techniques I've learned to present in a powerful and winsome way, then the audience will relate. It is hard to describe, but this connection is a tangible, substantial feeling for both speaker and audience.

Prepare until you are full of the information. Use the P.I.E.R. method. Develop your on-stage presence. Then smile and enjoy the opportunity to speak.

"IF YOU THINK YOU CAN DO A THING OR THINK YOU CAN'T DO A THING, YOU'RE RIGHT" ~HENRY FORD

BUZZ WORDS FOR SUCCESS

Three other factors play a significant role in making each presentation a success:

WHO ARE YOU?

The person you are becoming matters when you are communicating from the stage. Each of us is a work in progress. God's goal for your life is not who you are or what you've accomplished. His primary concern is who are you becoming.

Ask yourself, "Who am I becoming?"

My natural tendencies are to be bossy and decisive. I am becoming a team player and one who considers the opinions of others. I am becoming a person who listens to everyone's opinion before I state any opinions or decisions. Over the years, I have changed my personal definition of success. From a desire to be a corporate star and receive a large paycheck to a person who wants to reach her potential and glorify God in all she does. Changing this characterization of success so drastically requires me to ask questions of myself each day. Do I trust what I say on stage? Do those in my family and close to me see good in me, or is my on-stage persona a fake? How much of how I live and what I say is authentic?

I developed a monthly questionnaire for myself. At the end of each month I use my calendar for the previous month and review how I behaved at events and on the phone and internet as I assess my spiritual growth. Here are the questions I ask:

Category: Humility—needs of others first

1) Question: Did I experience any struggle with a sense of pride this month?
2) Rate my humility patterns this month from 1-10: _____

Category: Integrity—doing the right thing, regardless

1) Question: Was there any situation this month where my words didn't match my actions?
2) Rate my Integrity patterns this month on a scale from 1-10: _____

Category: Truth—keeping it real

1) Question: Did I exaggerate or alter the facts to make myself look better?
2) Rate my Truth patterns this month on a scale from 1-10: _____

Category: Loyalty—faithfulness to family, friends, and organizations

1) Question: Did I utter any words or take any actions that hinted of criticism or dissatisfaction this month?
2) Rate my Loyalty patterns this month on a scale from 1-10: _____

Category: Submission—respecting my authorities

1) Question: Have any words or actions indicated an independent or rebellious spirit this month?
2) Rate my Submission patterns this month on a scale from 1-10: _____

Category: Passion—fervent drive toward the cause God has given me

1) Question: Is my passion for God's calling on my life currently fresh or stale?
2) Rate my Passion patterns this month on a scale from 1-10: _____

Patience—a high degree of tolerance for other's mistakes

1) Question: Were there any unhealthy indications of impatience in my interactions this month?
2) Rate my Patience patterns this month on a scale from 1-10: _____

Love God—fully surrendered to the direction and will of God

1) Question: Have I walked in full surrender this month?
2) Rate my Love-for-God patterns this month on a scale from 1-10: _____

Love People—responding in a Christ-like manner

1) Question: Have I treated everyone as Jesus would treat them?
2) Rate my Love-for-People patterns this month on a scale from 1-10: _____

Persistence—have I stayed on task even when it was difficult?

1) Question: Am I experiencing feelings of discouragement or desire to quit?
2) Rate my Persistence patterns this month on a scale from 1-10: _____

I complete this analysis each month because I want to know:

What is God asking me to pay attention to today?

Why do I struggle in a particular area?

What is one step I can take to grow in this area?

As I review my calendar and the activities I have participated in this month and the people with whom I have interacted, I asked these questions while the month is still fresh on my mind. I am brutally honest with myself so that I have the chance to grow from this exercise.

To keep myself on track toward my personal definition of success, I work through my evaluation questions. It isn't fun or exciting; it is hard work. But scrutinizing my month in this way changes me and helps me follow my calling.

WHAT ARE YOU OFFERING?

The second factor that goes into finding your sweet spot and making successful presentations is your theme. My overall message theme is joy, so my presentations must have elements of optimism and confidence. I want all my messages to reflect this attitude of joyfulness because life is an adventure to be faced with courage and faith—and a bit of fun. If I communicate this potential in my presentations, then I have offered my best. Perhaps your message theme is recovery. If so, your life story, and your presentations, should reflect it. If your message is about the power of prayer, then you should be a person of prayer.

What Emotions Will You Communicate?

Audiences will feel an emotion when you speak. If you don't intentionally guide them to feel a specific emotion, one will take over and dominate your presentation. You can guide them to feel joy or encouragement. Or your presentation might inspire guilt or fear. I remember hearing a presentation on the dangers of imported meats. I left the meeting afraid to eat a hamburger. The speaker didn't give us any hope or tips on how to choose healthy foods.

I never want a person who has heard me speak to leave the session with apprehension or fear, especially since I speak often about spiritual issues and matters of the soul. I want to give my audience the opportunity to walk out of the auditorium or event center with an overwhelming feeling of joy. If I do my job well, then I can accomplish my goal.

Christian Speakers Find the Zone

For preachers and teachers with a Christian message, there is a zone that is supernatural when God gives you words that you didn't expect to say. His Holy Spirit within you as a believer will show up. Your job is to prepare, pray, research, and train, and He will give you what the audience needs to hear. He doesn't put words into your mouth unless you have done the hard work of Scripture memorization and investigation into the details of your subject combined with much prayer, study, and research. Once, when I was teaching a weekly Bible class, I was amazed at the words that came out of my mouth. I had been privately memorizing a large section of Scripture, the first nine chapters of the book of Acts. The memorization attempt was a personal discipline that I wanted to do privately, and I told very few people about my memory project. As I was teaching my class, I remembered a few verses from Acts chapter 3 that applied perfectly to the topic. I had no plans to use those verses as a reference for that day's lesson, but because I stored the words away in my mind, God called them up at just the right moment.

Luke 4 tells us that the Spirit led Jesus. I know I can find my anointing when I am led by the Spirit of God to do what God has asked me to do, even if I don't understand why. Even if it doesn't fit into my plans. Even if it doesn't make sense to me.

USE YOUR WORDS WELL

You can speak as if God's words are yours when you know your calling, prepare fully, and watch for the connection with your audience. But training matters. Sometimes when a person approaches me at the end of a presentation, they ask how they can become a speaker too. My reply usually surprises them. I tell them that speaking is a craft that must be learned. I suggest they get training. I say the messages are planned, and every gesture and voice and facial expression is planned and practiced. I tell them there are no careless, empty words.

Use your words well. Only then can the Holy Spirit do His work as you speak. Become a devoted, passionate follower of Christ; present messages that center on your life's theme and give answers and hope to your audiences.

CHAPTER 17
UNCOVERING THE GEMS

WORDS HAVE INCREDIBLE POWER. THEY CAN MAKE HEARTS
SOAR, OR THEY CAN MAKE HEARTS SORE.

~DR. MARDY GROTHE

My pastor gives great sermons. It is clear he has prepared for each presentation with great care, and he presents truth in an interesting and inspiring way. His sermons contain gems—sentences or phrases that stick to my mind so well that I carry them with me, and eventually the statements become a part of how I live. Some ideas become so ingrained I dare to write and speak about them. One of those most powerful statements from him is, "God isn't interested in giving you a tweak; He wants to transform you."

The contrast of the statement is stunning and convicting and encouraging all at the same time. The twist in the logic is dramatic, and the use of the word tweak is just enough slang to give the hearer a little jolt. The phrase is a precious gem from his sermon. I speak about this statement. I've written about this statement. I talk to my friends about this statement. I encourage my grandkids with this statement. I live this statement!

"THROUGHOUT HUMAN HISTORY, OUR GREATEST LEADERS AND THINKERS HAVE USED THE POWER OF WORDS TO TRANSFORM OUR EMOTIONS, TO ENLIST US IN THEIR CAUSES, AND TO SHAPE THE COURSE OF DESTINY. WORDS CAN NOT ONLY CREATE EMOTIONS, THEY CREATE ACTIONS. AND FROM OUR ACTIONS FLOW THE RESULTS OF OUR LIVES." TONY ROBBINS

When you are preparing your presentations, work on your vocabulary and craft well-worded sentences and phrases that convey the powerful points you want to make. Never find satisfaction with mediocre language or stories. Organize your speech and craft your statements. Make the presentation so interesting the audience will be on the edge of their seats to hear what gem you will give them next.

When I hear or read a phrase that touches my mind or heart, I try to find a way to repeat the phrase or word as soon as possible. I tell the next person who calls me about the phrase. I tell my husband or my kids about what I read. I write a note or an email or a text to someone using the phrase. Each time I repeat the phrase, I embed it into my mind, so it becomes a part of me.

This week, my husband read aloud a story from a book he is reading. The story was about a man who took a safari and hired porters to carry the supplies into the wild. The first day they traveled fast through hard terrain. The next morning, the man was eager to get started early, but he couldn't get the workers to get up and get moving. When he asked why, they said they were waiting for "their souls to catch up with their bodies." I repeated the phrase several times. He and I both used the phrase during the day as we talked about us being at this beautiful retreat center on a writing retreat. We are waiting for our souls to catchup to our bodies because of our busy and frantic lifestyle. Later I told the phrase to a friend who called. Then our daughter and granddaughter came by for a visit, so we told them about the phrase and what it means to us. Now I'm writing about it to you. That phrase will become part of me, and I will use it as a gem in future presentations because I have rooted it into my mind and heart.

Craft sentences and phrases in your presentations that will become someone's gem. If you hear or read a gem, plant it in your mind by repeating it or writing it on a list. These gems will inspire and challenge your audiences.

Emily Dickinson said, "I know nothing in the world that has as much power as a word." You and I must use precise language – not words that are kinda what we mean. We sometimes settle for the most common, boring words, lazily falling back on our limited language when we could work harder and find the perfect word to convey our meaning.

One place to find great language is in reading good literature and good writers. Consider reading or re-reading the classics to increase your vocabulary. Think of every word you plan to say in your presentation. Is there a stronger verb or a more descriptive noun that would say it better? Your goal is not to impress the audience or to find unfamiliar words; your goal is to express your thought with the best word.

"SPEAK CLEARLY, IF YOU SPEAK AT ALL;
CARVE EVERY WORD BEFORE YOU LET
IT FALL." ~OLIVER WENDELL HOLMES

When I am working on a presentation, I play with the words in my points and stories and instructions, trying to determine which word would be better, what twist I might put in the phrase to strengthen it, or how I might change a sentence's structure to get the most impact. Consider the following techniques to revive and reinvigorate your content.

PAUSES

Nineteenth century English author Martin Fraquhar Tupper said, "Well-timed silence hath more eloquence than speech." Your best moment in your presentation might be the moments when you don't speak. If the timing is right, your silence will speak volumes.

A pause gives your audience time to catch up with your thought. A quiet gap allows the power of your words to sink in. A break in your sentence lets the audience consider the result … sometimes when the moment of silence is over you can share what they figured out or you surprise them with a different conclusion.

If you have been talking about the busyness of life—showing how your day is filled with running back and forth and errands and trips in the car and responsibilities—your pause along with a sigh or deep breath will lead the audience to the idea that living at that pace is exhausting. You never have to say how exhausted you feel, but your audience will feel it.

When you tell a story, a long pause just before the final line might make a difference between the audience understanding how the story makes your point. In one of my presentations about viewpoint, I tell about the words of a little girl when all the adults in the room were frantic with worry. The audience always laughs when they hear the enthusiastic upbeat words from the child. I wait in silence until they look up from their laughter, then I say: "The girl has perspective." That moment of silence is powerful.

Silence is a key component in humor. A perfectly timed pause can make a story funny, but without the silence, the humor might fail. I sometimes tell an audience about my unique grandmother name. It goes something like this:

When I found out I was going to be a grandmother, I learned that we get to pick out our grandmother name. I liked that idea and began a quest to find the perfect name. I rejected some names such as Granny—although I think it is perfect for some people, it didn't seem to fit me. I also rejected Big Mama—for obvious reasons. I finally settled on using my initials KP as my grandmother name. I was comfortable with the moniker because many people already used it, and I also thought it sounded hip and modern.

Do you know that K is a really hard letter for toddlers to say? Do you know that P is a really easy letter for toddlers to pronounce?

Then I pause. I let those two questions sink in. I let them guess what my cool-hip name became. I twist my face to show my humiliation and chagrin. Then I say, "You guessed it; my name is PeePee." The audience howls, and I have developed a great rapport with them. The story would not be as effective if I didn't use that pause to let them think.

I use that story as a connection builder so that the audience will relate to me. It doesn't fit for every audience, but often works well. After the event, dozens of women will come to see me so they can tell me their funny grandmother name. I've heard some doozies.

Use pauses to make the audience think and silence to set up a powerful statement or punch line.

QUOTES

Quotes from famous or successful people provide heft and offer a valid reference for your point. A quote is most powerful when you quote it in a dramatic or powerful voice, and is least powerful when you have to read it to the audience. If the entire quote doesn't fit your point, eliminate the distraction by using only the part that applies. If one phrase or part of the quote makes your point, don't distract from it by giving the part of the quote that doesn't fit.

Earlier in this chapter, I quoted Emily Dickinson. The quote I used was only part of a longer quote. "I know nothing in the world that has as much power as a word. Sometimes I write one, and I look at it, until it shines." Because we are talking about speaking, I didn't use the second part of the quote. Dickinson was a brilliant writer, and her focus was on writing, but her statement about the power of a word is appropriate in speaking.

Practice speaking the quote aloud so you can present it with power and clarity. Practice using pauses in various places in the quote. Practice emphasizing different words. Be sure you can pronounce every word with clarity.

Read this quote from Tom Stoppard's *The Real Thing: A Play*.

> "Words ... they're innocent, neutral, precise, standing for this, describing that, meaning the other, so if you look after them you can build bridges across incomprehension and chaos. But when they get their corners knocked off, they're no good any more ... I don't think writers are sacred, but words are. They deserve respect. If you get the right ones in the right order, you can nudge the world a little or make a poem, which children will speak for you when you're dead."

The quote is an example of a quote that I could use as an example in this chapter. It speaks of the power of words and how getting the right ones in the right order could change the world. I love the quote, but I won't use it in a speech. It is too long. It brings in concepts that might get my audience off track, such as words being sacred; words needing respect; and poems, which children will quote. You will lose the attention of your audience if you use a quote that is too long and too complex. Pare it down or don't use it.

While it is important to give attribution to the person you are quoting, emphasize the quote not the person. Add an adjective to describe the person such as Author … or Philosopher … or Poet … or President … A long explanation of who said the quote might distract from the quote–unless the story associated with the person fits your point.

Verbal Gems

Like finding a diamond in the rough, we can polish and carve words using tools that bring out the beauty and value. Use one of these tools to strengthen your sentences.

Rhythm

Consider the pace and fluidity of your sentences. Determine the mood or emotion you want to convey to your audience. Create rhythm by increasing or decreasing the tempo of a statement. If you vary the length of your sentences, you will create variety instead of monotony. The hearer moves with the ebb and flow of your words. Read the sentences aloud to notice how the words connect to each other. If you stumble or hesitate as you read it, rework the sentence. Rearrange or remove words or phrases that don't work. Add descriptions using strong verbs and even stronger adjectives. Remove adverbs, especially any that end in "ly."

When you speak, you will naturally stress certain syllables. Be sure your stresses fall on the content words. Each of these stressed syllables becomes a beat of the rhythm. Change the pitch of the stressed syllable for variation. Increase the time or the volume of a beat to emphasize it.

Look at this sentence from Psalm 46:10, "Be still, and know that I am God."

Read it aloud, emphasizing different parts of the statement.

Be still.

Be still and know.

Know that I am God.

Now read the entire sentence, emphasizing different syllables. You will discover the best rhythm for your voice.

Repetition

Repeating words or phrases in a presentation is a verbal device to bring attention to an idea and to keep the audience engaged. Using a word or phrase a few times to keep it in the memory of the hearers.

Successive Clauses

Repeating the same words as the beginning of several connecting sentences creates familiarity and adds to the persuasion of the thought. The repeated phrase has a different ending in each statement. This technique is often called anaphora and has been used in famous and iconic speeches you've heard or studied.

WINSTON CHURCHILL—

"We shall fight in France.

We shall fight on the seas and oceans.

We shall fight with growing confidence…

We shall fight on the beaches.

We shall fight on the landing grounds.

We shall fight in the fields and in the streets.

We shall fight in the hill.

We shall never surrender…."

MARTIN LUTHER KING –

I have a dream that one day this nation will rise up and live out the true meaning of its creed…

I have a dream that one day on the red hills of Georgia, the sons of former slaves and the sons of former slave owners will be able to sit down together at the table of brotherhood.

I have a dream that one day that even the state of Mississippi…will be transformed into an oasis of freedom and justice.

I have a dream that my four little children will one day livein a nation where they will not be judged by the color of their skin but by the content of their character.

I have a dream that one day down in Alabama…little black boys and black girls will be able to join hands with little white boys and white girls as sisters and brothers.

Using repetition is a powerful tool if used well. Repetition is easily found in poetic works and it enhances and enriches your presentations.

Flow

Your audience will join you if your speech flows. If your presentation seems disjointed and choppy, the audience may tune out or become distracted. The tools for creating a smooth flow to your presentation begin with pacing yourself. I frequently hear a presenter who will spend more than half (sometimes two-thirds) of his allotted time setting up the speech. He might tell how he got interested in the topic or how he researched the material or why the information is important. By the time he has gone over all the reasons we should listen to the speech time has passed, and the speaker only has about five minutes to cover all the points of the outline.

A clock or watch can help you stay on pace. A well prepared and pruned introduction will allow you to get to the meat of your message quicker. One tip is to write a sentence of 8-10 words that summarizes your presentation. If you can't concentrate the message to a few words, you are not prepared well enough to give it. Communications coach, Diana Booher, said, "If you can't write your message in a sentence, you can't say it in an hour." Strong words, but critical to the flow of your presentation.

Cadence

Think of the metronome your childhood music teacher used to help you stay within the beat of a song. Every speaker needs to develop an internal gage to produce a pleasing vocal cadence. Nervousness causes some speakers to rush their sentences, but enthusiasm can push a speaker's cadence too far so that the person sounds more like a cheerleader than a presenter. If you speak too fast, your audience will not track well, and most audiences will miss your main point. Unfortunately, most will stop listening rather than struggle to keep up with your fast pace.

I've coached some speakers who go to the other extreme because they are too measured and calculating to rush. These speakers drag the stories out, think too long between sentences, and bore their audiences. Some in the audience will think, "get on with it!"

Studies show that variety in cadence is the most effective method in speaking. The musical quality causes audiences to pay attention. Some sentences need to be spoken quickly, and some need to be intentionally slowed down for effect. This pattern creates a more interesting presentation—one that is easy to listen to.

Cadence is difficult for you to hear for yourself. You will need help. A coach can provide an evaluation and show you how to develop the skills you need. A group such as a toastmaster's club can give feedback regarding your cadence. Recording yourself either in audio or video is useful to help you hear your potential tempo problems.

When you hear a presentation, pay close attention to the cadence of the speaker. Do they speak in short sentences with pauses between the sentences? Make notes about what worked and didn't work for that speaker. Determine what style and technique would be comfortable for you to use in your presentation.

What is Your Twist?

When I am working on a presentation, I often start off with the facts I've researched and studied. I can prepare my presentation with this information, but when I'm finished, I realize it sounds like boring facts or worse, sounds condescending (do what I say) or preachy (you are doing it all wrong). Informative, but not inspiring. If you have a succession of Do and Don't sentences in your presentation, you are at risk of sounding haughty or pompous.

To fix this issue, I concentrate on the take-away value of the talk. What do I want the audience to learn, or how do I want them to take action? Understanding the benefit for the hearers brings me to another question: Why do I want to talk about this subject? Have I learned from this topic? Has my life changed because I know this information? What is my personal experience in this area? What is my twist?

Here are some hacks for discovering your personal viewpoint of a topic and what you want the audience to see or learn or change.

1) Write a 20-word sentence describing the talk. Then cut the sentence to 10 words.

2) Trim the excess. Minute details may seem important to you, but a hard analysis reveals most of the extraneous details do not matter to the audience.

3) Explain how the information you want to present affected your life by telling a personal story as your example. If learning these facts caused you to change a habit or attitude, tell the audience.

4) Show the audience how to implement the new information into their daily life.

5) Stay true to your main point—the bridge—and do not wander off topic.

You can create a twist in your presentation by using contrast and comparison—assets vs flaws; daily vs weekly; past vs present; strong vs stronger. A twist can often be found in presenting both sides of a story: management is concerned about one part of the manufacturing process, but labor is concerned about a different aspect. Or some scholars interpret this passage as being history and some scholars interpret it as end times prophecy. Putting yourself into the shoes of the person with the opposing viewpoint will create a contrast.

Focus on the emotion that you might create in your audience. Will they laugh? Will they cry? Will they laugh until they cry? Do you want to spark empathy or joy or enthusiasm or action? Knowing your goal for the audience will help you add the perfect twist.

Read every statement you intend to make in your presentation to determine how you can add fresh language or powerful imagery to make the sentence more poignant and challenging.

Metaphors and metaphoric language help present the twist. One way to give your content a makeover is to use an overarching analogy to brush your presentation with color by comparing each feature or point of your presentation to an item familiar to your audience. (Notice how I used a makeup metaphor in the previous sentence by choosing verbs and nouns to relate speaking to cosmetics. But a cosmetic metaphor isn't a good choice for an audience of men. So, you might choose a rock-climbing analogy.) In each of your points, choose nouns and verbs that relate your content to elements of rock-climbing.

Whatever metaphors you choose, be sure to keep it consistent throughout your presentation. Don't make a rock-climbing analogy for your first point, then a gardening analogy, and then a sewing analogy. If you mix metaphors, your audience will get confused and your presentation will seem unfocused.

Good Orators

Occasionally, on the political scene in America, a figure will emerge who is exceptional in oratory. John Kennedy had extraordinary skills. He used a contrast in one of his inaugural speeches. "Ask not what your country can do for you, ask what you can do for your country." These words not only ring true to the spirit of America, but the tempo and cadence of the phrases linger in our ears.

Ronald Reagan was a master communicator who used his skills as a trained actor to modulate his voice. He knew when to speak loudly, when to soften the phrase, and when to pause. His challenge to Mr. Gorbachov about the Berlin wall echoes through the years: "Tear down this wall!" Such a short sentence and simple words, yet it is filled with power and strength. Reagan mastered storytelling. It is said that his speechwriters wrote the major policy points he needed to make and then wrote, "Tell a story here," in his speech manuscripts. He was so adept at telling a story that made the point they didn't have to prepare it for him. Your audiences are accustomed to stories from books, magazines, TV, radio, and movies. They love to relate a principle to a story.

CHAPTER 18
WOULD YOU LIKE THAT
"TO GO?"

"THE SUCCESS OF YOUR PRESENTATION WILL BE JUDGED
NOT BY THE KNOWLEDGE YOU SEND OUT BUT BY WHAT THE
LISTENER RECEIVES." ~LILLY WALTERS

Focus on the audience when you speak. The greatest tool you have in your speaker tool kit is the "take away" that you give to the audience in each presentation. Let's consider all the gifts you have for the audience.

INFORMATION.

Even if your presentation is primarily inspirational, be sure you give some new tidbit of information for each person to learn. I mentioned in an earlier chapter that a good presentation is often 70% inspiration and 30% information. That format is a worthy goal, but make sure you spend as much time or more in preparing the smaller percentage. The information should be fresh—including new facts the audience may not have known before and new perspectives on facts they already know. Don't fall back on clichés or tired quotes. Instead, find new ways to communicate the information—stories (especially personal stories), questions, humor, visuals, videos, new metaphors, new twists on old clichés. Never use a technique gratuitously.

Information can take the form of prescriptive instructions ... how to use a day-planner; facts about a situation or product ... what makes our product superior to the competition; or proof of a point of view ... six evidences that Noah's Ark existed. But information—no matter how creatively you present it—will not reach the heart of the audience unless you give them the "why" of the facts. How is knowing these facts going to change the way I schedule my day, choose this product, or understand God's love? What does this information mean to me? How will it change my life or perspective or attitude?

Encouragement.

How can you take what your audience already knows and show how they can reach new heights that are bigger, better, and more fulling than their wildest dreams? Your presentation may be the tipping point—the final gentle push—that a person needs to help him or her step up to a new level. Maybe he will start a new venture, or she will finally stand up for herself, or he will decide to trust God completely because of your encouraging words.

What have you built into your presentation to reassure someone in your audience? What reinforcements have you given the audience? How have you cheered them on to new heights?

Challenge

Lives change when your audience puts the points of your talk into practice. What will stay with them after you have left town? And I don't mean items they bought from your table at the back of the room. I'm talking about something deeper.

If you are speaking to a business group, then help them see how their product (their widget) can help consumers live a better life. Most corporate marketing departments are savvy enough to articulate how company products can change the lives of users, and you can find that information on their websites. Depending on your audience and the reason you were invited to speak, you will want to think specifically about how you can help them do something better, faster, or cheaper. Sales teams, for example, frequently need motivation and inspiration, so you will want to give them a take-away that creates those feelings and leaves them with a plan of action for the next time they feel discouraged.

If you are speaking to church leaders, then give them a new vision for their neighborhood. I know of one church who accepted the challenge of a speaker to reach their neighborhood for Christ. They surveyed the homes around the church and learned that the neighborhood had changed dramatically to a new ethnic dynamic. The church changed the style of its worship services, offering music and programs that fit the community. They hired bilingual pastors and held prayer walks throughout the neighborhood. The changes in their neighborhood were dramatic. The message of Jesus was the same—they just used new methods. The speaker had challenged them to change, and they did.

Take-Away Keys

How do you build in a take-away when you prepare to speak? Your work begins with a strong foundation—your content and purpose. To explore potential take-aways, ask yourself these questions:

What truth do they know?

What truth can I show them?

What truth will change their lives?

Then use the Word of God and your personal experiences to answer these questions. What can you say to challenge the audience? What illustrations or stories will stir their hearts, challenge their current actions, and create in them a desire to change? How can your message touch them in a deep place to give them hope for the future?

When I speak on the friendships of women, for example, I like to include loyalty. I know from experience that the audience hasn't thought deeply about how this attribute is essential to friendship. I show them the importance of loyalty by using an event from my life. I discovered the value of loyalty, or lack thereof, when someone I thought was my friend was not loyal to me.

I had helped this person and promoted her to a prominent position in the organization. Later, when something didn't go well in a project, she didn't take my side. Instead, she blamed me. I was heartbroken and felt deeply betrayed by her lack of loyalty.

So when I speak about loyalty, I describe how loyalty matters and how a friend stands by her friend when rumor or circumstances condemn. When (not if) I make a mistake, my true, loyal friends are still my friends. And even when I do wrong, rebel, or fail completely, my loyal friends may confront me privately, but publicly they will stand by me. Non-loyal friends make themselves scarce.

Then, as I talk, I take the concept further with the audience. I challenge the group to make a commitment to each other. I ask them to look at a friend and say aloud, "Dear friend, I'll be loyal to you even if the evidence condemns you." Saying the commitment sentence to each other helps the women in the audience make a life-changing decision to be loyal—a commitment they "take away" with them.

Often you can leave a "challenge" take away with the audience by giving them a great quote that will stick with them. If you use the quote within a story, it will make a bigger impact. In one presentation I tell the story of a pastor who was so kind to me in the hours just after I found out that my father had passed away. I describe him and the place I saw him and how he responded to me. And then I quote what he said to me, "Karen, I don't know how you feel, but I care how you feel." That kind sentiment helped hold me together during the next weeks of facing the loss of my beloved father … someone cares. That sentence has an enormous impact on the audience when I share it, and I often get letters or emails from people who have claimed the quote for themselves or used it when comforting others. My pastor's words have impacted thousands with a challenge to respond to others who are hurting.

An application or "take away" is the how-to of real-life, real-time issues, and concerns of the audience. The best moment in a presentation is when a listener glimpses how your point fits into his or her own life. Good speakers watch their audiences for that moment—then stop to explain the idea more deeply and more clearly. If a concept or lesson has some sticky points, then clarify it lucidly. Doing so calms the fears of those in the audience who tend to question everything. For example, if you are teaching about praying big, bold prayers, then take time to explain the difference between having courageous trust for provision vs treating God like a candy store.

Call to Action

To help your hearers move from where they are when they enter the room to the alternative way of thinking, understanding, or doing, requires a call to action. Webster's dictionary defines "take away" as a conclusion, but I am sure the benefit that an audience gets is much more than a verdict. As the speaker, you need to give them an appeal to act that will change them or move them or cause them to know. To make this kind of call to action, you will need to frame it in a winsome way:

Bargain – Assure the audience that the tips, guidelines, or information you will present will succeed.

"If you follow the advice, I'm going to give you in the next ten minutes, you will save at least $1000 before the end of the year."

"Do you want to spend more time in meditation and develop a successful quiet time so you can hear God's voice in your life? I am going to show you how."

Risk – Give evidence that your method or approach to a problem is worth a try.

"These healthy eating tips will increase your energy and help you reduce the number on the scale. What do you have to lose?"

"Trying these leadership tips is the certain way to build your team without jeopardizing your role as leader."

"These reliable techniques for building your social media presence cost nothing and are risk-free."

Proof – Show the audience that you believe in your message so strongly that you know it will work in their lives too.

"I guarantee that paying attention to the nuances that move your credit score up or down are guaranteed to help you make financially sound decisions in the future."

"These methods are guaranteed to change your attitude about exercise."

Give It A Try – Help the audience see that they can make the changes or implement the guidelines or follow their dreams if they will begin now or go all out for the result they want.

"Give God a year."

"In a year from now, you'll be so glad your started today."

Change – Ask your audience to adjust one area of life in order to achieve success in another area.

> "Cleaning and shining your kitchen sink first each morning changes your desire to keep your counters clutter free."

> "Using a daily reading guide will develop new dedication to read the Bible through."

> "Planning a menu for the week changes your expectations for dinner plans and reduces the number of times you go for take-out each week."

Let's Do It – Challenge your audience to take action to accomplish new goals.

> "Let chocolate be your cue for making new friendships."

> "When you see a rainbow, remember the promises of God."

> "From now forward, make every Monday your planning day."

Your goal as a speaker is to inspire your audience so that they will never be the same again because they heard you speak. That is "take away." Your goal is that they will say, "I'm going to try it," or "I can do it."

Give More Than They Expect

Give the audience much more than they paid for and more than they expect.

The people in our audiences desperately need inward healing, and they are looking for answers. They are asking, "Can you help?"

While none of us has a magic wand, we can give our audience hope, answers, solutions, encouragement, steps, action points, instructions, and real concrete help.

For example, an audience may come expecting to hear a presentation on personality types. The speaker could give a powerful speech on the subject and give the audience what they expected. But if the speaker adds a spiritual component, for example, to the personality facts, then the audience will be given a new understanding. As a speaker, give laughter, stories, facts, but also give the deeper aspects associated with your topic.

As you work on your presentation during the preparation stage, go through the material looking for places you have offered more than they bargained for. Decide how you will emphasize those places in your speech.

Give More of Yourself

One of the most important qualities of a speaker is how you relate to the meeting planner and those who have hired you to speak. Having a servant's heart is another way to give more than the group expects. Although you are the speaker, be willing to help in any way you can.

You become part of their team the moment you step off the airplane. Think and act like one of the team. If they are setting up tables, grab a table and help. If they are spreading tablecloths, you take a few. If they are decorating tables, pick up a few centerpieces and place them on the tables. I can't tell you how many times event leaders have said, "you don't have to help, you are our speaker." I always reply, "I'm on your team and I'm here to help." You can move tables and chairs. You can also pray with those who are distressed and hurting. Never lose your desire to help and to help right now.

CHAPTER 19
REACH EACH

"IT IS NOT TRUE THAT EVERYONE IS SPECIAL. IT IS TRUE THAT EVERYONE WAS ONCE SPECIAL AND STILL POSSESSES THE ABILITY TO RECOVER IT." ~CRISS JAMI

Frequently, before or after your presentation, members of the audience will line up or congregate near you, wanting to talk to you. When you speak (especially in Christian events), do your best to respond to these people. Don't manage the entire crowd as a unit. If there is a long line, then focus on each person in front of you individually—not the person down the line who might look more interesting or less needy. As you are with one person, don't look over the shoulder of that person at something else. That gives the impression that you would rather be anywhere but there.

TOUCH INDIVIDUALS, NOT CROWDS

At the end of events, folks stand line to speak with me, sometimes to tell me about a difficult situation in his or her life. Whether the problem is physical illness, job crisis, family difficulties, or personal tragedy. My response must be relevant and kind—and appropriate. Though I'm not a professional counselor, a practicing physician, or a psychologist, I have options when dealing with a distressed person.

1) I listen. Pay attention to the person; look them in the eye and don't allow distractions around you to pull your eyes away. The technique of listening with your eyes takes practice and determination. Just talking to someone who listens might be the healing balm the person needs.

2) I am kind. As a fixer personality type, I could give a solution or a quick fix for the person's problem. More often than not, the person isn't looking for my advice. Words of kindness are more valuable to a person in need.

3) I encourage. A few words from me which help them take another step or face another day. Help the person see light in the darkness and positive in the negative.

4) I pray. Praying for the person on the spot is often curative and restores hope.

If I sense a bigger need, I refer the person to local doctors, pastors, or counselors rather than offering medical or psychological advice. I usually discuss this concept with the event planner ahead of time and ask that he or she have a qualified person standing by.

Deal with each issue one at a time. Don't worry about the person who just left or the person you will talk to next. Make the person in front of you feel as if he or she is the only person in the room. Ask for the person's name and then use his or her name at least once while talking. Work on your memory skills so you can remember people, names, faces, events, and situations in case you see them later in the day or the event. Then you can respond with grace.

My friend Florence Littauer was a master at making each person feel important. Her eyes never left your face. She asked significant questions and made you feel she cared. Every person in the crowd who lined up to talk to her left the room thinking, She likes me best!

MINGLE BEFORE AND AFTER

Mingle with people and learn something about them. If you do this before your talk, then it will help you know and understand your audience. If you do it after your talk, then it will help you reinforce your take-away for those audience members who are still undecided or confused.

If you teach a regular group, then invite them to your home and find out about their family and life. Hospitality like this isn't common in our fast-paced society. When we lived in The Woodlands, Texas, we started a weekly Bible study class that grew from four to about seventy-five people in a short time. I love to cook and entertain, so we hosted Sunday lunch at our house for class members and others who were part of the church but who we didn't know well. Every Sunday, we had ten to twenty people for lunch.

The reactions we received from people when we called to invite them to lunch were sometimes comical. They would ask, "Why?" because the art of hospitality has been lost in the hurry-up of life. Some people assumed we had ulterior motives, and we were going to push them to join some multi-level, get-rich-quick pyramid scheme, but the rewards of getting to know people were rich and satisfying.

When you speak, do everything you can to get to know the event planners, the team who invited you, and the members of the audience. You are not a hand-shaking politician; you are a servant. You may not solve all the world's problems, but you can get involved on a deeper level with people and find out what they are facing. You can care, and you can pray.

I often quiz myself: Do I have compassion on the people in the audience? Do I see them as they really are? People loved by God? The crowd may look different from me; they may be different politically or have differences of opinion on social issues, but I still see them as sheep needing a shepherd. And I love them.

Pay Attention

People need attention, and they need to know that you notice them. Once, when I was the teacher of a large weekly class, I worked hard, making sure the meeting happened in an orderly manner. The class had grown so fast that we hadn't had enough time to organize leadership and enlist others to help with the physical details, such as setting up chairs, preparing handouts, making coffee, and all the other details of getting ready for the class. One morning I was doing all this work. I had a long list of tasks to complete before the group arrived. But a woman coming into the room interrupted me. She was sobbing.

"What's wrong?" I asked.

"Are you mad at me?" She said.

I put my arms around her shoulder. "Of course not. Why would you think I'm mad at you?"

"You just went past me in the hallway without even speaking to me."

I was stunned. In my focus on completing my checklist, I had rushed down the hallway past her. I hadn't even seen her. She felt completely ignored, with good reason.

I was focused on a good thing, (getting the classroom and materials ready), but I failed to minister to one of the folks I was teaching. Be willing to see and reach out to those around you even when you are on an important mission. You may need to get your microphone on or talk to the event planner about the lighting, but as important as your mission may be, the people are more important.

Maintain a Ministry Mindset

Look around. See the people at the event. Care about each one. Go to the event early to set up microphones and stage and lighting. Prepare so well in advance that you need not make any last-minute changes to your notes. Ask the event planner for a schedule with starting and ending times, so you can plan time to mingle with the crowd.

As You Speak – Take Your Cues

Maya Angelou said, "People will forget what you said, people will forget what you did but people will never forget how you made them feel." Will they feel encouraged, challenged, or enthusiastic when they leave your presentation, or will they be overwhelmed and feel there's not much hope? Your job as the speaker is to "Find out what's keeping them up nights and offer hope. Your theme must be an answer to their fears."

The only way to achieve this kind of emotion in your audience is to know your audience and connect with your audience. Study your audience to determine the issues they face. Be aware of their mood or what may have gone on in their lives earlier in the day. Think not just of surface problems, but also of deeper life issues. What is the culture of this part of the country? What are the trends in this area? What is the economic and social situation? Who are these people? What brings them together? What divides them? Once you've answered these questions, you'll be able to give value and benefit for your audience to enjoy during your talk and to take away.

How to Connect to the Audience—Mistakes and Fixes

MISTAKE #1: You seem too perfect, too successful, too still.

FIX: Mingle with the crowd before the event without telling them you are the speaker. Meet people. Be authentic and regular with them. Go around the room as they come in and make them welcome.

MISTAKE #2: They don't know why they should listen to you?

FIX: Promise a benefit. Either with promotional materials or in the program description. Or as you mingle say, "We are going to have some fun today." Near the beginning of your talk, tell them what benefit they are going to receive: "If you listen to these tips, I promise to revolutionize your exercise routine forever." Do whatever you can to make them feel excited before you take the stage. Colorful handouts. A small trinket related to the topic. A discount coupon for your book at your book table.

MISTAKE #3: They don't know what to do with the information you gave them.

FIX: Give clear action steps for when they return home. What shall they do to get happiness, joy, money, to declutter, to find time to rest?

MISTAKE #4: They are overwhelmed with all the "do" and "don't" steps you've given them.

FIX: Tell more stories that illustrate how to accomplish the new ideas you've given them.
Stories will seal the deal for them. Give them examples of what they can do when they get home.

MISTAKE #5: They don't relate to you.

> FIX: Involve the audience. Ask questions during your speech. Be spontaneous. One way is to start with a question: "How many of you have been in a hurricane? (works in the South or East Coast). "Who is a grandparent?" Or ask a question followed by a laugh-line. "How many are moms? Followed by the laugh line: "Who has a mom?" "Who exercises? Followed by the laugh line, "Who has thought about exercising?"

MISTAKE #6: Your presentation feels stale

> FIX: Perhaps you've given this talk too many times. If so, freshen it up with recent stories, new instructions, new references. Turn the talk upside down so you won't sound tired. If you are bored, they will be wearied too.

Giving a presentation is never about whether they like you or about filling up your allotted time or getting through the material or impressing the audience. The presentation must be about the audience. Obsess about your audience. Did they connect? Will they benefit?

AUTHENTIC

One author said, "My story is more about failures than success— far more." That's the kind of story I want to read or hear because if the speaker seems perfect and pristine, I find it hard to relate. One person told me recently, "when I saw you before you spoke, I was impressed by the poised, put-together person I saw, but while you were speaking, I realized you are a normal person who faces the same problems I face." Our audiences must see that we are on the journey with them. If we have failed and started again, so can they.

Allow your audience to see that you don't have life figured out. Tell them about your mistakes and the times you took backward steps. They will love you for it. If you are perfect and only brag about your successes, they won't believe you nor will they relate to you. Don't be afraid of your flaws and disappointments. One speaker told about her divorce and the pain it caused. She had many stories of situations that led to the day of the breakup and beyond. As she told the story, she mentioned how she was kind in the face of abuse and how she made right choices and how much she prayed and could forgive. A better way to explain a hard situation is to own your mistakes and failures and show the audience how you blew it too. If you forgave, help the audience see that it was a battle and a result of grace and tough choices to be kind.

The C. A. T.

One tool helps me focus on the audience: the C.A.T. method. A Bible teacher who influenced me used this method. When I start my preparation, I put these three letters at the top of my first page of research. C.A.T. The letters stand for Cause the Audience To: _____. In that blank, I state what I want the audience to learn or do because they heard this speech.

Do people need to hear it is not the same as do people want to hear it. When I know my audience—who may be faith-based, business based, students, senior citizens—I can find the CAT quickly. Ask these questions about your audience:

What are the ages in the audience?

What are their interests?

Why are they attending the event? (required or voluntary)

Are these people leaders?

What is the mix of cultures, viewpoints, status?

Knowing these answers along with knowing the theme of the event provides crucial information for building the presentation.

Audiences are perceptive. They know if a speaker is authentic and sincere. How well you know your audience and how well you deal with any distractions or unusual happenings will help them feel relaxed enough to become open to absorbing your message. Handle yourself with grace, with laughter (especially at yourself if the occasion arises), with genuine concern, with wit, and winsomeness.

"MAKE SURE YOU HAVE STOPPED SPEAKING BEFORE YOUR AUDIENCE HAS STOPPED LISTENING." ~ DOROTHY SARNOFF

NEVER MIND THE DISTRACTIONS

During a recent contemporary church worship music time, a bat began swooping about the large darkened room, throughout the audience, and then up above the stage. As it dive-bombed the worship leader's head, he exclaimed, "What is that?" But he recovered quickly, adding, "Let's rock the bat!" The audience laughed and sang with gusto.

Distractions will occur. Smoke, fire alarms, loud claps of thunder, crying babies, fainting audience members, plus situations we can't even imagine will happen while we are speaking. When they do, our reactions will guide the reaction of the audience and the affect it has on them.

You can't ignore interruptions, so respond to them with poise and kindness. Your audience will appreciate the relief that acknowledgment brings. If the lapel microphone pops and cracks with static, then simply change to a hand-held microphone with no comments or work a quick reference to it into your presentation: "Trouble is everywhere, even in microphones." If you are calm and composed during a disruption, your audience will be unruffled.

If your messages are interesting enough, the audience will listen no matter what happens. Use stories, visuals, and terminology to which they can relate. Make every story compelling enough to cause the audience to want more or to go deeper into your subject, as the disciples did with Jesus, always asking for more. Your audiences will ask for you to return. Individuals will be inspired, for example, to attend Bible study, or get into a Bible reading program on their own. Lives will be changed.

Speak to the Personalities

Your audiences are filled with four different kinds of people.

The first group is the fun-loving, excitable, outgoing, popular sanguine personalities. These people are ready to have fun and will engage with you if you tell stories and add wit and humor to your presentation. You can recognize them by their colorful clothes and their assorted facial expressions as you speak. Be sure you give them colorful descriptions and interesting stories and creative, colorful handouts with pictures.

The second group is the organized, controlled, introverted, perfect melancholy personality. This person will pay close attention, will follow your logic, and will want to understand the message more than they want entertainment. You can recognize them by their neutral clothes and their close attention to your handout. They are the ones with pads and pens, taking notes so they remember what you say. Be sure you speak carefully and give all the answers to any fill-in-the-blank sections of your handout.

The third group is the strong, opinionated, hardworking, powerful choleric personality. This person wants to know you are qualified to speak and wants provable facts. Most of all, this personality type wants action steps to take when they go home. Help them implement the life-changes you propose.

The fourth group is the hardest to recognize because these people are calm, easygoing, and do not stand out in the crowd. They will listen and even like what you say, but they probably don't want to fill in blanks on a handout. And they don't want to work hard when they leave. Give them permission to relax by giving them small steps they can take and then help them see the benefits of change.

In every presentation, try to add elements that will resonate with each of the personality types. That way you will give something to everyone. No one will be left out. You might even use a little self-deprecating humor to poke fun at your presentation style and how your personality type delights one portion of your audience while it frustrates or disappoints another type of person. Then you can turn the tables and give another personality type what they want while pointing out that you are simultaneously boring another audience segment.

CONNECT TO COMMUNICATE

The individuals in your audience aren't interested in what you have to say as much as they are interested in connecting with you. If you lose the focus of your message, your presentation will be words alone. If you focus on the audience and what they need and think they need, your presentation will be communication. Consider how the main point of your message will make a difference to the audience next week, next year. Your audience may not say it aloud, but each one secretly asks, "So what?"

CHAPTER 20
THE CARE AND FEEDING OF A
HEALTHY PLATFORM

THE LONGER THE SPEAKER'S BIOGRAPHY — THE LESS
EXPERIENCED THE SPEAKER.

As you think about building your platform and marketing your career as speaker, remember the most important marketing lesson: Anything that works today will change. Technology changes. "What's hot" today may not be hot tomorrow. The types of messages that create responses changes. So, what do you need to do? Learn as much as technology and social media as you can learn. Get help to understand your computer, the social media platforms, the styles of communication, and become proficient. A few years ago, I would have told you to learn all there is about FaceBook and Twitter because that's all you need right now. But in today's climate, it is most important to know where your audience hangs out. Is it FaceBook, Twitter, Instagram, LinkedIn, or some other new social media platform? You should set up an account on each platform whether or not you are using it often. Try to use the same name (or at least very similar) on each platform. A potential event planner may see your name on Twitter and search to see if you are on Instagram by searching your name. Your goal is to have a presence on each platform, so you'll be ready when that platform becomes the next favorite of your audience. Having a presence doesn't mean you have to post all the time on each platform. Pay most attention to the site you are targeting and post on the others occasionally, but regularly.

Creative genius and coach McNair Wilson said, "Disengage my self-worth from my itinerary." He's right and I would add, disengage your self-worth from your social media numbers. It is far better to have 1000 followers who you know and connect to than 100,000 who really don't know you. This makes your job on social media clear. Engage with the people who respond to any post you make. Reply to them and begin a conversation. If they get to know you by your engagement, they are going to be interested in your speaking (and writing).

On Stage

If I want the audience to know about my books and products at the back-of-the-room table, I have two options. One is to talk about and show the books during my presentation—like giving a commercial break. The other option is to provide a handout with book descriptions and benefits to each person attending. A third option is to have someone else talk about the books and products on the book table—also like a commercial. I prefer the promotional handout rather than the up-front commercial, but the commercial may work better for you. My caution would be to tell the audience what is available on the book table and present it like a commercial—rather than trying to put in not-too-subtle references to your books or products into the speech itself. I have seen speakers read from their book—conspicuously (and awkwardly) holding the book in front of the audience. Other speakers have referred to their book ad nauseum during the presentation. "In my book, I say …" "I put those tips in my book…" I think the audience sees through these not-so-subtle attempts at selling. Better to present the commercial straight up before you speak or after you speak.

Gaining a bigger audience and becoming more well-known is not for your personal recognition. The more people you speak to, the more you can accomplish what God has called you to do.

Go where invited. Every opportunity to speak is an opportunity for you to grow as a person and improve your speaking skills. I want to use the gifts God had given me. When you do the same, you'll be surprised how He will build your platform.

When I first began speaking, the opportunities were few, and I promised God I wouldn't say no to any opportunity to speak. So, today, I do my best to go wherever the opportunity presents itself, and I try to work out the details. Finding your sweet spot and operating within the boundaries of that special connection that you alone can have with an audience is the mark of genuine success when speaking, not large crowds or large fees.

Large or small crowds, big honorarium or not, I try to go wherever and whenever I am asked. I am willing to teach or speak or pray or work. Are you?

Make the Effort

Building a platform takes effort. Your audiences will grow if you care about the individuals in the audience and if you give well-prepared, value-added presentations. What you do for the good of individuals, no matter how small or how few people see it, will pay off by expanding your success with larger and larger groups.

Join In

At most events, I try to participate in whatever the group is doing. If they are having a style show or doing a mix-and-mingle activity or small groups, I join in the fun. When I attend a small group, the attendees feel as if they have made a new friend in me.

I also like to look for people I can encourage. Spotting hidden talent is like finding buried treasure. Because I coach speakers, I am always on the lookout for people who seem to have a knack or gift for speaking. I often see someone who has great potential to speak briefly to the group. At one event, I listened intently as one woman gave a short presentation. She was a natural and had the audience's rapt attention. Later that evening, I pulled her aside and quietly told her I saw something special in her abilities and that I thought she should pursue a speaking career. She was so moved that I singled her out. She and I have stayed in touch for several years, and I've loved following her progress as she follows God's calling. I don't pass out these kinds of compliments casually, and I didn't speak to her publicly for show, but I encouraged her so she may make a Kingdom difference as she follows her dream. Sometimes all it takes to change a person's life is one well-timed compliment.

Stay Humble

No one likes to be around people who continually talk about themselves and brag about their house, car, kids, money, skills, or spiritual gifts. No matter the size of your platform, do the ministry associated with being the speaker in as private a way as you can. Besides, it can be such fun if you mingle with the crowd before the event and get to know them, laughing and enjoying each other's company—then see their surprise when you are introduced as the speaker.

It should be enough for us to see people changed. We should not want them to point to us to give us fame, recognition, and glory. Don't revel in or repeat any praise you get. Just serve the needs of the people, encourage those God places in your path, and help in any way you can.

Start Small at Home

The best place to grow your audience is at home, in your town, in the venues that are closest to you. You need a place where you consistently speak, teach, or present. Look for a weekly Bible study group, a home group, or a class that challenges you to give fresh vital information on a consistent schedule. Your skills will grow. Your confidence will soar. Your abilities will shine. Can't find one? Start it yourself.

Be ready to speak. Build a repertoire of on-the-spot presentations you can give in one minute or five minutes or ten minutes. Your testimony could be the topic. No matter the length, make sure it has a great opening and closing. Memorize the verses that go with it. And be ready. First Peter 3:15 says, "Always being prepared to make a defense to anyone who asks you for a reason for the hope that is in you." Be ready. You will gain a reputation as an interesting and powerful speaker, a speaker who can present on short notice. You will become a go-to speaker.

As you build these impromptu presentations, include simple, compelling, interesting stories. People in the audience will want you to come to their town or group. Craft the stories well. I have a message on perspective that is built around one story. I can give the message in one minute, three minutes, or thirty minutes, depending on the needs of the event. Audiences appreciate the message because I have used the techniques in this book to craft an effective opening, tell a perfectly formed story, and conclude with a well-planned and challenging ending.

When an emcee or program director says, "We'd love to have you say a few words today," I ask how many minutes I have. Then I tell the story and the points in exactly that time. The program director appreciates and remembers how professionally I handled the short notice and the time allotted. The audience enjoys and learns from the well-designed words. Members of the audience go back and tell their program directors at home, and I receive more invitations to speak. Your platform grows when you give value.

Build an Internet and Print Presence

As your ministry grows, you will want to create a website that is easy to navigate and looks professional. Make your speaker page inviting. The website should tell event planners what you will do for them and how you will help them be a success. Write a short biography about yourself, starting with today and working backwards. Don't start with where you were born and then give a blow-by-blow detail of your life. Only include facts in your bio that are relevant to your speaking career.

Prepare printed materials too. These materials should reflect who you are and what you offer. To be most useful, your printed materials must contain:

- ☐ Your name (You'd be surprised how many forget to include their name.)

- ☐ Your contact information (I recommend obtaining a post office box, rather than giving out your street address.)

- ☐ A short bio

- ☐ Some personal tidbit of information, so people can relate to you

- ☐ Information on some topics you speak about. Give the topic a clever title. Write a short paragraph with three elements. First, create a hook sentence to interest the person in the topic. Second, write a sentence or two about the content of the presentation. Third, end with a line or two about the take-away, or the benefit, for the audience.

The look of your printed materials and your website should reflect you, your personality, and type of presentations you give. Are you delicate and flowery? Are you sophisticated and modern? Are you all business and no fluff? Make sure your colors, fonts, graphic design, and overall feel of your promotional material reflect who you are.

Market and Promote for More

Want to know the top eight ways to get more speaking engagements? A speaker friend and I did an unscientific survey of our past year's speaking appointments—more than 100 events. These are the top eight ways we got these jobs:

- [ ] Postcards
- [ ] Word of mouth
- [ ] Spin-off events
- [ ] Speaking for free or low fee
- [ ] Friends
- [ ] Speaker to speaker
- [ ] Speaker bureaus
- [ ] National conventions

Send postcards to targeted churches, businesses, and organizations. Get the name of the person in charge of event planning and follow up with a phone call. Be sure your postcard tells event planners what you will do for them, how they will benefit, how you will make their job easier, and how you will make them a more successful event planner. You can also send postcards to a general zip code which will not be as personal but will generate some responses.

Word of mouth and spin-off events happen when you do so well at one speaking event that people can't wait to tell their friends or invite you to their next event. Such enthusiasts often create new events just so they can invite you again.

Speaking at free or low-fee events gives you the opportunity to practice and you gain recognition. Consider business groups, service clubs, professional organizations, health groups, women's clubs, MOPS, and education and parenting groups. All these groups are looking for speakers. The more you speak, the more your name will become associated with the experts in your field.

Friends and other speakers who refer you are the best promotion for your career. One sanguine lady with friends in many places heard me speak and enthusiastically recommended me to others; she has been instrumental in booking dozens of additional events. Join speaker bureaus if they fit your needs and attend national conventions of church or industry groups to keep your name in the forefront.

ONLINE VALUE

Systematically set out to promote your speaking career. Use Twitter, Facebook, blogs, websites, and other online sites to make your name well known. The best method is not to tell the world how wonderful you are. Instead, give out valuable information. Provide tips and guide sheets and advice and instructions that will help people. When you post online and give value, your name becomes synonymous with your subject and if you do it well, you will become one of the go-to experts in your field. The reality of the Internet is that people search it for information. They do not want to be given a sales pitch, nor do they want to hear all about you. They are interested in what information and help you can provide to them. They will come back to your blog or follow you on Twitter or Facebook or Instagram if you give out value. If you are only promoting yourself, they will not pay attention.

Collect the names and email addresses of everyone who attends your presentations. Offer something of value to everyone who will give you his or her email. One friend offers a tip sheet to be sent out by email to all who sign up. Another speaker asks attendees to sign up for the newsletter she emails once per quarter. Another speaker collects names and email addresses and has a drawing for a door prize at the event.

Marketing yourself and building a platform are part of speaking.

Decide how you will make your name known and pursue the online and printed avenues that will get it done.

Chapter 21
Blueprints for Team Building

LIGHT IS THE TASK WHERE MANY SHARE THE TOIL. ~HOMER

You should pick a team to help you. You cannot do alone what you must do. Choose reliable people and then share your vision in such an inspiring way that they will give you the much-needed help you crave.

Pour into Your Team

As the leader, give your team lots to think about and cast a new vision and a higher standard to live by. Love your team and pour yourself into them by counseling them privately and teaching them as a group. Bring them along with you on your speaking journey by giving them reports on events and asking for specific prayers. Train them for the tasks you need. Help take their lives to a new level of maturity and service.

Consider how you will influence those closest to you – your ministry team. Give your team the opportunity to make forever changes through teaching and mentoring.

Time Together

It is your responsibility to teach your team and not to expect them to do what you want without a clue from you. Model mentoring to them and show them your best. Help each one work inside their personality. Teach them what you have learned. Coach them to write, to speak, to preach, to teach, to serve. Leave a legacy of people. If you have followers, give them jobs. Send them out to do the job. Give instructions and guidance—where, how, what to do if rejected.

A student is not above his teacher, but everyone who is fully trained will be like his teacher.

Ask these trusted people on your team for council. Does my talk have any shaky theological points? Do I seem or have I said anything that might be insensitive? Is the point of my message clear?

How To Choose Your Team

Choose hardworking people willing to invest time in your ministry. Don't pick people who are trying to make a name for themselves and want to ride your coattails.

When choosing a team, don't be afraid of the one no one wants you to choose. That person who seems like an unlikely choice may be exactly who you need. A strong choleric personality who may be loud and who expresses opinions with too much brass; or a quiet melancholy personality who analyzes the downside of every idea; or the giddy sanguine who seems too flippant; or a quiet, calm, phlegmatic personality who seems disinterested may be best for you and your ministry.

On Your Team You Need:

☐ A Celebrator – a person who believes in your destiny and applauds the journey. The most likely candidate for this team position is a sanguine personality. Who else celebrates like a sanguine! Be sure you choose one who has enough choleric to stay focused on your ministry.

☐ An Encourager – a person who will strengthen your spirit. As one of the spiritual gifts, encouragement can come from any of the personalities. A choleric will coach and assure you. A sanguine will be your loudest and most exuberant cheerleader. A melancholy will carefully choose true and helpful words, and a phlegmatic will surprise you with depth and wisdom because when a phlegmatic speaks, he or she always has something worthwhile to say.

☐ An Admonisher – a person who will notice when you've taken steps down the wrong road and who loves you enough to correct your path. A choleric is a superb choice for this job because who else loves to offer correction? But be sure your choleric admonisher has some softness either from his or her secondary personality or a big helping of the spiritual gift of mercy or the fruit of the Spirit's kindness.

☐ A Planner – a person who looks into the future and sees where your ministry might lead; a person who sees the big picture and will to help map the future. A melancholy's outstanding organizational skills and thoughtful creative ideas or a phlegmatic with a contemplative thought process make good planners.

☐ An Intercessor – a person who wages spiritual warfare on your behalf. Any personality type might be an intercessor for your ministry. The phlegmatic and melancholy will not forget to pray, and the choleric and sanguine will pray fervently.

☐ A Mentor – a person who has traveled the road ahead and will share wisdom. Find a mentor with your same personality type who will help you operate in your personality strengths.

☐ A Counselor – one who will assist you through personal dilemmas. A phlegmatic or melancholy will listen to your predicaments and help find solutions.

Ask God to bring these team members into your life either by invitation or through divine encounters. With team members like these, your ministry will grow and blossom, and you will stay on the right path.

CHAPTER 22
A CLEANSING BREATH

"LIFE ISN'T ABOUT FINDING YOURSELF. IT'S ABOUT DISCOVERING WHO GOD CREATED YOU TO BE." ~DR. CATHERINE HART WEBER

As I develop my speaking and writing skills, I must develop myself. The two are tied together. If I am responsible for the depth of my life, I can allow God to be responsible for the breath of it.

It is critical to take time away to refuel, refresh, and reinvigorate your life and your ministry. In one of the busiest weeks of his life (Luke 4:42), Jesus got up before everyone else to go out to pray. He had been traveling, choosing His disciples, preaching, serving, ministering—imagine how He might have wanted to sleep in to stretch His human body and snuggle down into the covers. Just a few more ZZZZs. But He went out to pray before daybreak.

A quiet time is important to you. Life seems too busy to have the opportunity to be quiet. A quiet time is important – not for study or work, but for prayer and quiet and contemplation.

In the speaker life, you will have failures and rejections. Sometimes you won't be accepted or will be misunderstood. Sometimes the message you planned won't work. I once spoke at a conference with many speakers. My time slot was right after lunch on the third day. Everyone was exhausted and had just eaten a large meal. My allergies were flaring up, and I had taken some strong antihistamines and felt numb. On top of all those facts, I was giving a presentation that was new and complicated, and I didn't have it as clear in my head as I usually do. It didn't work. I never connected with the group and many of them dozed off. What a miserable time for me. And them.

Sometimes you will face a group that has issues like I did at a retreat in the mountains of an eastern state. The church was in the midst of a split, and the women were warring. One table laughed through every session, enjoying their own little jokes and clique. Another table cried the entire three days. When these kinds of events happen, you need to move on. Keep your heart and soul focused on Jesus, and you will survive these tough situations.

A Daily Place

Do you have an isolated place? Do you go there to meet Jesus? Do you pray and read and meditate there?

Find a spot in your home where you can be with Him every day. A room that is calm and restful. A chair that is comfortable. A place to keep your supplies such as pencils, markers, notepads, journals, a Bible to write in, prayer journal, prayers to pray, thoughts to meditate on, and verses to memorize. Go to that isolated place even if you are tired or busy—especially if you are tired or busy. For me, this means getting up before everyone else. I love the quiet and calm of the early morning. I love my favorite chair, and with a beautiful cup filled with fragrant coffee, I say, "Good morning, Lord." He always meets me there. Where is your quiet place? Did you spend time there today?

PRUNING

When we built our dream home on some acreage near Montgomery, Texas, we chose the top of a small hill for the house. So, the landscape company had to build up the front steps and walkways. They built four levels with flowerbeds. The first spring, I planted Mexican Heather in the lowest beds and also a bed of this favorite flowering bush near the house. That winter, we had several ice storms. When spring came around again, the plants were brown and looked dead, especially on the lower level. I put my clippers almost even with the ground and clipped the brown bushes down to about one-half inch, hoping there was still some life under the ground. When I worked my way up the levels to the bed near the house, I saw that because the plants had some protection by the house, the leaves were yellow but not brown, so I only trimmed off the ends as I shaped the plants. In a few weeks, the plants at the bottom were beautiful, dark green leaves and bright purple flowers, but the plants near the house were still a sickly yellow and had no blooms. The difference? Radical pruning.

One of the important principles of the New Testament is the principle of pruning. We need to be pruned. Bad habits need to be identified and cut out. Pain must be resolved. Work on your craft. Watch yourself on video. Listen to yourself on audio. Work on the skills of speaking. Take courses. Read everything. Get a coach. Do whatever you need to do to get better each time you speak. What point or story or example is weak or doesn't really fit? Which point or statistic or quote is so cumbersome that it slows the message down?

Not only must you and I be willing to prune our messages, we must also be willing to be pruned personally. Are you willing to allow someone to critique your messages? Will you gladly ask for advice and cheerfully accept correction from someone you trust?

A Scheduled Time Away

Several times a year, you and I need to get away for a time to renew. Have you ever gone to a silent retreat? It is a remarkable experience. I attended one in San Diego at a monastery high atop a hill overlooking the ocean. We had a teacher who challenged us to spend long periods of time alone with God with no talking, working, or other distractions. Each of those several-hour-long segments of silence was life-changing for me as I learned to listen to God. I attended another silent retreat in Pennsylvania; each person stopped talking at seven in the evening on Friday and didn't speak again until Sunday afternoon. I discovered God has much to say if I will be quiet.

Life coach Jerome Daley encourages us to consider a recurring sabbatical when we regularly schedule time away from our normal schedule, time we can unplug and listen.

God is the one who established a created order around recurring rhythms, from the daily rotation of the earth to our annual circuit around the sun and every rhythm in between. This pervasive reality begs us to establish our own rhythms of soul care. While there is no one-size-fits-all, consider an approach to rest and Sabbath that looks like this:

- ☐   One hour a day
- ☐   One day a week
- ☐   One (extra) day a month
- ☐   One weekend a quarter
- ☐   One week a year

Don't get confused. This is not vacation; this is soul-cation. What does one do for soul care in times of Sabbath or sabbatical? Here is my recipe: refresh, reflect, and refocus. In that order.[iii]

Have you considered a sabbatical? I think Jerome's suggestion is one we should grasp and implement.

Time every day and recurring time away and alone will help you grow roots. Pray, read, learn, journal, study, grow. Each time you do, you will become more like Jesus.

May all these techniques and tips help you AMPLIFY! all your presentations.

I'd love to hear about it. You can email me at kaeporter@gmail.com.

MEET KAREN

Author/Speaker

Karen Porter is an international retreat and seminar speaker and a successful businesswoman. She is the author of seven books.

Karen spends most of her time coaching aspiring writers and speakers and training communicators across the globe.

Karen is a frequent guest on regional and national radio and TV programs. She contributes to national magazines such as Focus on the Family, Discipleship Journal, and American Taste. She has also written curriculum for Lifeway Resources.

Business/Professional

Karen served as Vice President of International Marketing of a major food company in Texas for more than 30 years. She traveled around the world and her varied experiences (including dinners with Fidel Castro) contribute to the richness and depth of her writing and speaking.

Karen and her husband, George, own Bold Vision Books, a Christian publishing company.

Karen serves on the board of Classeminars, Inc, and on the national teaching staff. She also serves on the boards of First Place 4 Health, one of the nation's top health and nutrition programs, Fruitful Word Ministries, and Right to the Heart Ministries.

Personal

Karen says her marriage to George is her greatest achievement, but she'd love to talk to you about her five grandchildren! In her spare time, Karen continues her lifelong quest to find the perfect purse. Karen is a people person, plain and simple, and you will love to laugh with her and maybe even cry a little as she shares her joys and struggles.

(Endnotes)

[i] K. S. Wuest, Wuest's Word Studies from the Greek New Testament: For the English Reader (Grand Rapids: Eerdmans, 1997), Mk. 1:21-22.

[ii] Mac Davis, "It's Hard to Humble."

[iii] Jerome Daley, "Give Yourself a Break," Coaching the Coach by Georgia Shaffer, Bold Vision Books, 2013, page 272.

Made in USA - Kendallville, IN
1209932_9781946708533
12.09.2020 0959